FLOYD ON FIRE

FLOYD ON FIRE

KEITH FLOYD

BBC PUBLICATIONS
ABSOLUTE PRESS

CONTENTS

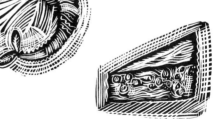

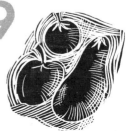

CONVERSION TABLES

All these are *approximate* conversions, which have either been rounded up or down. In a few recipes it has been necessary to modify them very slightly. Never mix metric and imperial measures in one recipe; stick to one system or the other.

WEIGHTS		VOLUME		MEASUREMENTS	
½ oz	10 g	1 fl oz	25 ml	¼ inch	0.5 cm
1	25	2	50	½	1
1½	40	3	75	1	2.5
2	50	5 (¼ pint)	150	2	5
3	75	10 (½)	275	3	7.5
4	110	15 (¾)	400	4	10
5	150	1 pint	570	6	15
6	175	1¼	700	7	18
7	200	1½	900	8	20.5
8	225	1¾	1 litre	9	23
9	250	2	1.1	11	28
10	275	2¼	1.3	12	30.5
12	350	2½	1.4		
13	375	2¾	1.6		
14	400	3	1.75		
15	425	3¼	1.8		
1 lb	450	3½	2		
1¼	550	3¾	2.1		
1½	700	4	2.3		
2	900	5	2.8		
3	1.4 kg	6	3.4		
4	1.8	7	4.0		
5	2.3	8 (1 gal)	4.5		

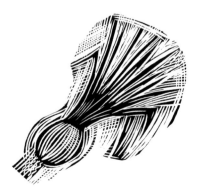

PREFACE

It was dark as I free-wheeled down Town Hill on that crisp Somerset Sunday morning. I leaned into the steep left-hander at the bottom and pedalled madly to maintain speed along the flat. By Milverton the sun had risen and the mist, defeated, revealed soft hedges heavy with nuts and berries, and orchards thick with hard red apples that I sometimes scrumped.

Just the swish of my tyres on the empty road. The dawn chorus faded as abruptly as it had begun. Past the house where the old lady had once caught me scrumping plums from the garden and into the lane which led to the lake. I climbed off the bike and propped it against a silver beech tree, unpacked my tackle and walked gingerly to the water's edge. Over the reeds which fringed the lake a huge fallen tree arched crazily across a patch of water lilies. A thicket of elder behind me, black with fruit, threatened to cause casting problems if I wasn't careful. The water was still and the bank shelved away gradually into soft mud. I could see the stalks of the lilies for yards ahead till the water turned dark green.

A shoal of fry spattered the surface in panic as a pike lunged at them. Eight o'clock. I rigged the tackle, threaded a bright red worm onto the hook and cast. The antenna float bobbed, dipped and steadied itself in the shadow of the fallen tree by the lilies. With an eye on the float I reached for my haversack and poured a mug of cocoa from my thermos. Hot and sweet. The float shot away. A minute later I landed a small perch with brilliant red stripes and put it into the keep net. Within an hour I had caught half a dozen – the biggest about 14 ounces. And then nothing. The perch had gone off the feed. I rebaited with stale bread soaked to a paste and tried for some bottom-feeding fish. Tench or bream perhaps. But the sun was creeping across the water and Mr Ratsey, the farmer, had said that fish wouldn't feed under those conditions. The float was motionless. The morning and my spirits were ebbing fast. And I was hungry!

The sandwiches were in my saddle bag, or so I thought. But when I opened it there was nothing. I had left them behind. All I had was a loaf of stale bread and a thermos of cocoa. Not much for a growing lad. I stomped around a bit till the solution dawned on me. I would cook the perch. Going home early was out of the question, so I despatched two of the perch, badly pricking my thumb on a dorsal spine in the process. I cut off their heads and fins and gutted them (there is a black ribbon which runs along the spine which must be scraped out). I cleared a small patch of grass and laid a ring of stones about 15 inches in diameter. I had no paper to start the fire but there were plenty of dry twigs around, and soon sweet wood smoke was spiralling into the Somerset sky as I piled on more substantial pieces to get the glowing embers I needed to cook. On either side of the ring I put another stone so that I could prop my ash spit above the fire thus preventing it from burning through while the fish was cooking. I sharpened the end of an ash branch into a point and skewered a perch onto it and placed it over the fire. I turned it every few seconds – I was afraid of it burning – and as I had no idea how long it would take I could not risk leaving it unattended for a second.

I did overcook it. But I munched every mouthful of the charred skin and dried flesh with relish. It was fabulous. The second fish was more successful – I got it crisp on the outside and moist within. To this day I swear it was better even than the perch *en papillote* that I ate in Lyon years later in a restaurant renowned for its perch dishes!

Trouble was I was still hungry, yet I couldn't face the prospect of cleaning another fish – to be honest, I didn't really like killing and was squeamish at the idea of doing it again. It was then that I had the inspirational idea of elderberry bread cakes, a hitherto unknown, and probably to this day little considered, gastronomic delight. I ripped out the heart of my stale loaf, soaked it in water and squeezed it into a paste and pushed in a dozen or so elderberries. I then flattened it in my hands to a sort of thick pancake and toasted it over the fire. I had browned one side when I remembered that I had seen some cob nuts in a hedge down the lane. I took the cake off the fire and collected a handful, which weren't quite ripe, crunched them open between my teeth and stuffed them in with the elderberries and toasted the other side. I admit it was a bit soggy in the middle but it tasted like heaven to a hungry fourteen year old!

Well, I have learnt a bit since then, although I must say that I would rather have that crude barbecue in preference to that charred disc of so-called meat that is all too prevalent these days. I love to cook outdoors and I hope this book will enthuse you as much as a burnt perch on a stick did me nearly 30 years ago.

Bon appétit.

INTRODUCTION

Albert Gassier is a big man. A sort of Gauloise-smoking Anthony Quinn. I was sitting in the bar sipping a coffee when he came in and offered me a drink. Which I accepted and paid for.

'I want,' he said as he sipped his pastis, 'to do you a favour.' I shuddered.

When Albert Gassier offered to do you a favour you accepted. No matter what it cost. I drew a Gitane from the pack and struck a match with my hand. The burning head broke off under my thumb. I winced and used his Zippo.

I looked across the bar. Léo was nonchalantly polishing glasses behind the zinc. Which was most unusual. I'd never seen him more than rinse them.

'I see.'

'Yes I want to make you some money.' His eyes narrowed as he leant over me. Clearly he had enjoyed garlic sandwiches for breakfast. 'Lots of money.'

'Lots of money?'

'Mucho dinero.' Léo was still polishing the same glass.

'How?'

'You know I have been building for many months. Plans, architects, bricks, drains. Planning officers. The mayor. Every day, every day telephone calls. Bribes, threats. Yes I have been building.' He lifted a hand towards the bar and the waiter refilled our glasses.

'So you see I am ready. They all said I couldn't succeed. But I have triumphed and everything is ready.' Albert drained his glass.

'So come to my office tonight at nine and I will explain.'

Nine o'clock in the soft evening before these mighty steel gates. I press the bell. Above the polished brass plate: A. Gassie, President Provence Antique Dealers' Association. Through a crack I see the yellow light of a low-wattage bulb illuminating the massive front door. Thick bolts slide silently back.

'Good, you've come. Follow me.'

I crunch across the gravel in my thin-soled shoes as cicadas chirp and cheep in the olive trees. Pale moon rising as the church clock chimes nine. Like a soul drained of hope tapping feebly on the iron door of the condemned cell. Through the high-ceilinged hall lined with longcase clocks standing like sentinels in the dim light. Past huge *armoires* and antique globes. I start at a stuffed bear in the gloom.

Albert Gassier in tartan shirt, jeans and slippers pushes a key into a lock that opens the door into the back garden, and beckons me on. Through a corrugated-steel sliding door into a huge brick-built hangar that smells of damp cement and toxic paint. I blink in the brilliant brightness as he pulls a switch that floods the cavernous hall with light.

'You see.' He points to the far wall. 'My pride and joy.' I stare over at a huge fireplace built three feet off the floor. 'This is where you will make your money. This is the covered hall for the antiques fair which will give us an extra 150 stalls, over and above those in the garden and the street. You will close your restaurant and run a barbecue for the duration of the antiques fair. I will charge you no rent, just ten per cent of the turnover. I can't be fairer than that. *D'accord?'*

'*D'accord*,' I said weakly.

It was late when I reached the apartment. I checked the answer phone and poured a Scotch and thought about the mess I'd got into. Grilling a few brochettes for friends on Sunday was one thing. Running a barbecue for the largest antiques fair in the south of France for nearly a week was quite another. The logistics were daunting. How many hamburgers a day? One thousand? Two? Never mind the steaks, chops, chicken and brochettes. How much charcoal? I lay awake pondering these questions till I fell asleep just before dawn. Only to be wakened by the demonic crashing and cheerful shouting of the refuse collectors, gleefully tipping the bins into the yellow lorry which blocked the narrow street outside my bedroom window.

I spent the day ordering hamburgers and meats from the butcher. He made the kebabs too. I discussed special rolls with the baker and ordered half a ton of charcoal.

The following day I humped trestle tables and folding chairs from one of Albert's many junk-filled stables and arranged an *al fresco* restaurant that owed more to the set design of a prisoner of war film I'd seen recently than to the charmingly rustic wistaria-enshrined scene I had originally envisaged. Still, with a few, borrowed potted plants and some tubs of geraniums it wasn't at all bad.

Cursing dealers were arriving with vans, trucks and lorries, blocking the entrances and exits in their selfish panic to be the first to set up stalls. Albert stormed in and out arranging places and threatening to expel malcontents – whose only crime was to ask for a power point or more space – and adding greatly to the chaos.

Priceless busts cheek by jowl with piles of rusting farm implements. Elegant rocking horses toppling on displays of porcelain. Men, stripped to the waist, struggled with massive pieces of pine furniture while their elegant wives tut-tutted and inspected their long fingernails, occasionally hissing out an 'Ooh-là-là' in a marked manner.

I made endless journeys to my restaurant with a hand cart to collect the fridges and calor gas cookers; to the *boulangère* to collect sacks of bread and to the butcher for buckets of pre-skewered kebabs. I was surrounded with cartons of paper plates and plastic glasses. I built a wall with wine cases, lit the fire, spread the trestle tables with paper and left the mayhem of the fair and strolled gently along the river to the nearest bar for a much needed pastis before facing the inevitable onslaught of starving *brocanteurs* at twelve o'clock.

I made a tin bath of salad and lit the gas under my desert rat-style chip-fryer. I was ready. The staff were briefed. Organisation had triumphed. Nothing could go wrong. Check the bucket of herbs, check the garnishes. Check the fire. Fingernails. Everything was OK.

Then they stormed us. Don't cook till you see the whites of their eyes, I shouted merrily as about 250 antique dealers engulfed us screaming for barbecued steaks. Well done! Bloody! Blue! With garlic! No fat! Without garlic! No fat! Without garlic! Without chips! With double chips! Me! Me! Me!

It was a memorable experience – and one never to repeat. Floyd on fire is one thing. Floyd under fire is quite another.

A WORKING ATTITUDE TO FIRE AND FUEL

Barbecuing is fun! That is the first thing that should be said, and said firmly. Of course it is important to grasp the essentials of the techniques involved, but not at the expense of the pleasure. So what follows is a simple and straightforward guide to the essentials.

TYPES OF OUTDOOR COOKING EQUIPMENT

1   Brazier

This is the basic type of barbecue, portable with detachable legs. The more sophisticated models have windshields or hoods and some come equipped with a rôtisserie.

2   Rôtisserie Grill

These grills have the facility for spit-roasting as well as grilling. The rack height is adjustable as is the height of the spit itself. This is a barbecue for serious outdoor cooks.

3   Permanent Garden Grill

The permanent garden grill is ideal for the barbecue fiend. There is something very special about cooking on a grill that is actually part of the outdoors. Make sure you position your construction at an angle to the prevailing wind and set the grate carrying the fire above a metal tray. This can then catch the ash as it falls and also provide good ventilation. Line the interior of the grill with firebricks. DIY kits for permanent grills are now available, so make a visit to your local garden centre for advice.

4   Hibachi

Very cheap to purchase but quite sturdy, this cast iron portable grill sells in thousands, year in year out. It comes in various sizes and specifications and is perfect for taking on holiday — along with a copy of this book, of course. Unlike the brazier type, the fire is laid on a grate rather than on the bottom of the firebowl, thus allowing air-flow under the fire which can be controlled by means of vents.

5   Hearth Cooking

When the summer has gone and all you are left with is a rusting barbecue on the terrace and fond memories of lazy summer

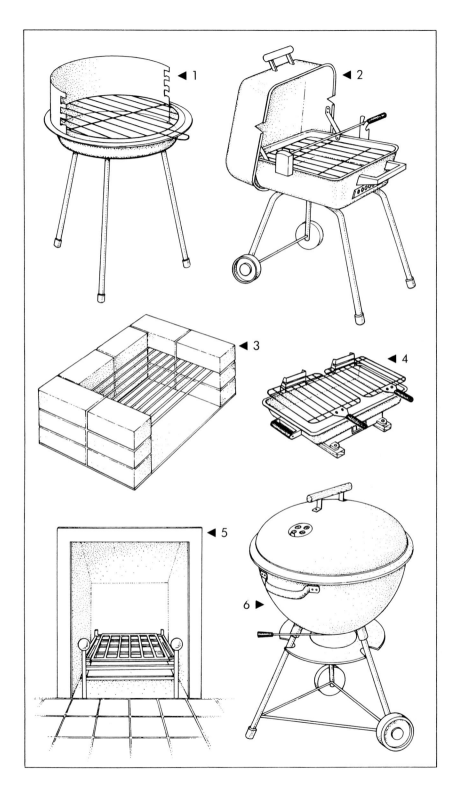

evenings spent sipping wine and munching fine-flavoured grills, console yourself with the fact that your hearth can now be the centre of attention, and your wood-burning feasts may continue through the long cold months ahead. A temporary grill can easily be erected over the embers of your fire, supported by a couple of sturdy bricks on either side. You can also pop food wrapped in tin foil into the dying embers at the side of the fire.

6 Kettle Grill

The kettle grill has a number of advantages over the more basic portable barbecues. The food is surrounded by heat and is cooked evenly and consequently at greater speed. Flare-ups caused by fat dripping onto the coals are far less likely, and food can be cooked even in the worst of weather conditions. Various types of kettle grills also incorporate a rôtisserie. The rack, however, is not always adjustable, so the heat can only be regulated by the use of vents.

FUEL

There is a variety of fuels on the market. Shun all charcoal substitutes and use only the finest lumpwood charcoal or high-quality briquettes. If you are lucky enough to have fruit trees in your garden, then the dried cuttings from these will make a superb aromatic fuel. Remember, artificially flavoured fuels are to barbecuing as pot noodles are to haute cuisine.

LIGHTING THE FIRE

The type of method used to ignite the fire depends very much on personal preference. Efficient methods include solid fire lighters, jellied alcohol and gas lighters operating off butane.

Light your fire by building a pyramid of charcoal. When the charcoal becomes covered in ash, spread the fuel evenly over the grate. The intensity of the heat can be varied by either separating the charcoal (to lower the intensity) or by pushing the charcoal together (to raise it).

THE DRIP TRAY

A quick word about the drip tray. The drip tray is an invaluable aid to cooking outdoors. Made of tin foil, it should be placed under the food to catch all the juices, which can then be either used to baste the food or as the basis for a sauce with which to accompany the dish. Surround the drip tray with charcoal, varying the amount, depending on whether you require a fierce and intense heat or a longer and more gentle cooking process.

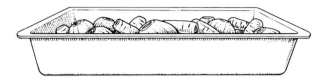

ESSENTIAL EQUIPMENT (see pages 24, 25)

1 Skewers (metal and wooden)
2 Small preparing knife for cutting out core of kidney etc.
3 Sharp cook's knife
4 Fish-shaped grip (e.g. bass, hinged)
5 Spatula
6 Basting brush
7 Tongs, various
8 Grip (for several chops, hinged)
9 Oven gloves
10 Ladle
11 Circular grip (e.g. sardines, hinged)

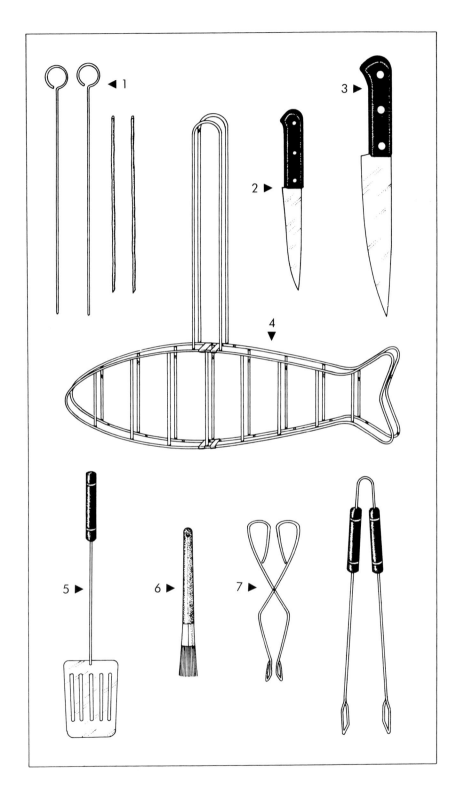

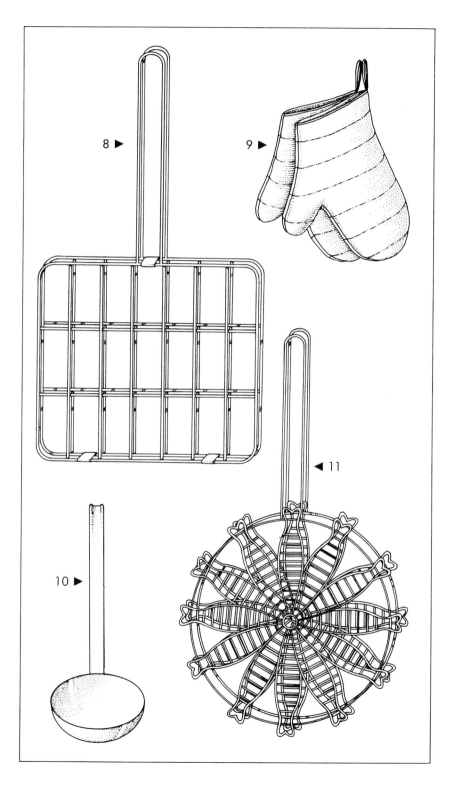

8 ▶

9 ▶

◀ 11

10 ▶

PREPARED BUTTERS MARINADES AND SAUCES

Savoury Butters for Grilling

A knob of any one of the following butters will cheer up the simplest piece of fish or any meat grilled on the barbecue. Just roll the prepared butter in the shape of a sausage, wrap in grease-proof paper or foil and pop into the fridge or freezer for use as and when desired.

Anchovy Butter

6-7 anchovy fillets
4 oz (110g) unsalted butter

Soften the butter and mash in the anchovy fillets.

Shrimp or Prawn Butter

2 oz (50g) unshelled prawns or shrimps
Dash of anchovy essence
Juice of 1 lemon
5 oz (150g) unsalted butter

Grind the prawns or shrimps in a food processor. Add the anchovy essence, lemon juice and the softened butter. Whizz in your machine till smooth.

Lobster Butter

2 oz (50g) lobster shell
Lobster roe
A little lobster meat
5 oz (150g) unsalted butter

Grind the lobster shell in a food processor. Add the roes, the meat and the softened butter. Whizz until smooth.

Maître d'Hôtel Butter

8 oz (225g) unsalted butter
4-5 tablespoons parsley, finely chopped
Juice of 1-2 lemons

Soften the butter. Whizz all ingredients in a food processor until smooth.

Wine Butter

4 shallots, finely chopped
7 fl oz (200ml) red wine
3 oz (75g) soft butter
Salt and pepper
Juice of ½ lemon

Heat the shallots with the red wine and allow the wine to boil away. Leave to cool. Now add the butter, salt and pepper and finally whisk in the lemon juice.

Herb Oil for Grilling

30 black peppercorns
6 bay leaves
3 sprigs rosemary
4 sprigs thyme
4 red chillis
4-5 sage leaves
½ teaspoon fennel seeds
20 coriander seeds
Best quality olive oil

Stuff all the dry ingredients into a 1¾ pint (1 litre) bottle, cover with the olive oil, whack in the cork and leave for a week or two, to use as and when you wish. The perfect oil for grilling.

MARINADES

Bigarade Marinade

Grated zest of ½ an orange
Juice of 1 orange
Grated zest of ½ lemon
1 glass Madeira
4 medium onions, grated
Pinch of cayenne pepper
1 teaspoon crushed black pepper
½ teaspoon salt

Mix the above together and marinate beef, pork, lamb or veal for 2 hours.

An Indian Marinade

1 teaspoon fresh ginger, grated
2 cloves garlic, finely chopped
1 medium onion, finely chopped
1 teaspoon cumin powder
1 teaspoon fresh coriander, chopped
½ teaspoon salt
A small tub plain yoghurt

Mix all the ingredients together and marinate your pork or lamb or whatever for 4-5 hours in a cool place.

Instant Marinade

This marinade is jolly useful for a spur-of-the-moment grill.

6 shallots, grated
1 teaspoon rosemary spikes
1 teaspoon thyme leaves
Salt and pepper
5 fl oz (150ml) cider vinegar

All you do is mix the above ingredients together and marinate your meat for 10 minutes on each side before grilling.

A Japanese Marinade

This is a very useful marinade for pork, chicken and chicken liver kebabs.

6 tablespoons sake (or sweet sherry or Madeira)
6 tablespoons soy sauce
1 teaspoon fresh ginger, grated
1 teaspoon brown sugar
1 clove garlic, crushed

Mix all the ingredients together and marinate your meat in the fridge for at least 6 hours. Dry the kebabs before cooking and once they are sealed baste from time to time with the remainder of the marinade.

Salt Marinade

This is an excellent marinade for pork. The meat can be left to marinate for up to 48 hours.

2 tablespoons juniper berries
5 allspice berries
1 teaspoon black peppercorns
1 tablespoon dried thyme
11 oz (300g) coarse salt
3 bay leaves, crumbled

In a large mortar grind the juniper berries, allspice berries, thyme and peppercorns to a coarse powder. Add the bay leaves and salt and grind until the ingredients are well blended.

SAUCES

Aïoli

As this is a barbecue book and most of the fun is to be had out of doors you are permitted to make this sauce the easy way.

8 cloves garlic
2 egg yolks
15 fl oz (400ml) best olive oil
Juice of 1 lemon
Salt and pepper

Put all the ingredients except for the olive oil into a food processor, turn on and pour in the oil slowly but evenly, until you have a beautiful, thick sauce.

Barbecue Sauce

2 cloves garlic
½ teaspoon salt
½ teaspoon paprika
4 tablespoons clear honey
3 tablespoons tomato purée
4 tablespoons orange juice
4 tablespoons white or red wine vinegar
6 tablespoons soy sauce

Crush the garlic and salt in a pestle and mortar. Then grind in the paprika, stir in the honey followed by all the other ingredients, one at a time, stirring all the while. Or you could whizz it in a food processor! Simmer the sauce for 5-10 minutes and serve hot or cold.

If you want a thicker sauce to use as a basting liquid, bring the sauce to the boil and then simmer gently until it reduces to the required thickness.

Béarnaise Sauce

This is a wonderfully versatile sauce which can be adapted as you want. For instance, just add chopped mint instead of tarragon when serving lamb.

½ glass white wine
2 tablespoons wine vinegar
1 shallot or small onion, finely chopped
Pepper
9 oz (250g) unsalted butter
3-4 egg yolks
1 teaspoon fresh tarragon leaves

Boil the wine and vinegar with the shallot and pepper until reduced by half.
    Melt the butter and keep hot.
    In a bowl, whisk the egg yolks. Reduce the speed of the whisk and pour the butter in slowly, whisking steadily all the while. Pop in the fresh tarragon and then whisk in the reduced wine and vinegar mix.

Green Piquant Sauce

Serve with shellfish and fish as well as meats and chicken.

4 tablespoons shallots, finely chopped
1 clove garlic, finely chopped
4 tablespoons parsley, finely chopped
3 tablespoons vinegar or the juice of ½ lemon
1 teaspoon anchovy paste or crushed anchovy in olive oil
½ teaspoon black peppercorns, finely crushed
3 pinches cayenne pepper
4 fl oz (110ml) olive oil

Whisk the lot together with a fork briskly till all the ingredients are well mixed.

Harissa

Harissa is a wonderful prepared chilli paste, extremely hot, which you can buy from oriental stores and some delicatessens. Use it sparingly like mustard, particularly with grilled offal.

Bass Flamed with Fennel and Armagnac (page 41)

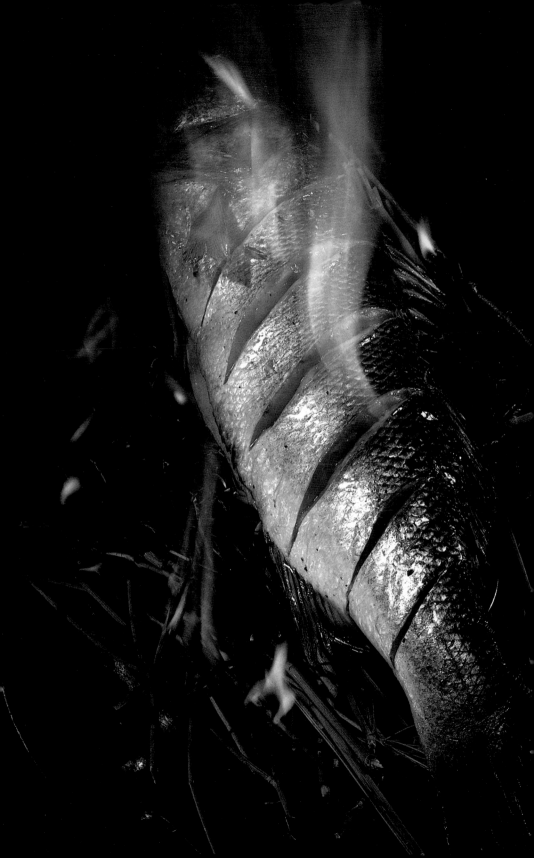

Hollandaise Sauce (the quick and easy Floyd way)

1½ lb (700g) unsalted butter
6 eggs
Juice of 1 lemon
Pepper

Melt the butter in a pan with a pouring lip. Put the egg yolks and whites with the lemon juice and pepper into the food processor and turn on. Pour the hot melted butter evenly into the whisking eggs until the sauce has thickened. To keep warm, place over a pan of recently boiled water until ready to serve.

Hot Horseradish Sauce

A sauce that goes very well with red meats and fish.

7 fl oz (200ml) double cream
2 tablespoons fresh horseradish, grated
Salt and white pepper

Gently heat the double cream for 3-4 minutes and then whisk in the horseradish, salt and white pepper and cook for a further 3 minutes over a low heat.

Lemon Sauce

2 teaspoons paprika
1 teaspoon sugar
1 teaspoon salt
½ teaspoon black pepper
¼ teaspoon dry mustard
Pinch of cayenne pepper
6 oz (175g) butter, melted
4 fl oz (110ml) lemon juice
4 fl oz (110ml) hot water
Tabasco sauce
2 teaspoons onion, grated (optional)

Stir the paprika, sugar, salt, pepper, mustard and a pinch of cayenne into the melted butter. Blend in the lemon juice, hot water and a few drops of Tabasco and the onion if required.

Mackerel Fillets Baked in Foil Envelopes (page 44)

Madeira Sauce

2 oz (50g) butter
1 oz (25g) flour
5 fl oz (125ml) chicken stock
2 fl oz (50ml) Madeira
Salt and pepper

Melt the butter in a pan. Add the flour, stirring all the while to avoid lumps, and cook till it turns golden but not burnt.

Now add the chicken stock, whisking all the while, and continue cooking for at least 5 more minutes. Now add the Madeira, salt and pepper. Simmer for 4 minutes more before serving.

Fresh Mango Paste

This paste makes a delightful accompaniment to grilled shellfish.

1 green mango
1 clove garlic, finely crushed
1 teaspoon fresh coriander, chopped
1 fresh chilli, finely chopped
Salt
3 tablespoons olive oil

Peel the mango, remove the nut and mash the flesh as smoothly as possible. Add the garlic, coriander, chilli and salt and finally beat in the olive oil till all is well amalgamated.

Nut Sauce

This nut sauce is great with white meat and fish, especially shellfish.

4 oz (110g) nuts (toasted peanuts, pistachio or toasted almonds – or all three)
1 clove garlic
5 oz (150g) butter
1 teaspoon anchovy paste

Crush the nuts and the garlic in a pestle and mortar.

Heat the butter in a pan and whisk it until it thickens to a cream. Now add the nuts and garlic and the anchovy paste and continue cooking and whisking for another 2-3 minutes and serve.

Mayonnaise

If you are planning to serve this sauce straight then you must use the best olive oil that you can afford. However, if you are planning to add herbs then a blander corn or nut oil should be used.

6 whole eggs, at room temperature
Juice of 1-2 lemons
1 tablespoon wine vinegar
Salt and pepper
1¾ pt (1 litre) olive oil

Break the eggs into the food processor and add the other ingredients, except the oil. Turn the machine to maximum for 30-40 seconds, until the eggs are really foaming. Now pour the oil in evenly and slowly for a couple of minutes. If by any chance the mayonnaise is too thick, turn the machine on again at half speed and dribble some tepid water in.

There will be enough mayonnaise to last you for a while, so pop it all into a bottle for use during the coming week.

Rouille

2 large cloves garlic, finely chopped
2 red chillis, chopped
Stale bread, soaked in water and squeezed out to the size of a large walnut
2-3 tablespoons olive oil

Grind the chopped garlic to a paste in a pestle and mortar – the quantity is too small for a food processor. Now pound in the nut of bread and the chopped chillis until smooth. Whisk in the olive oil until the mixture becomes like a smooth, shining red mustard.

Tartare Sauce

11 fl oz (300ml) mayonnaise, made with plain oil (see above)
1 teaspoon chives, finely chopped
1 teaspoon capers, finely chopped
1 teaspoon green olives, finely chopped
1 teaspoon parsley, finely chopped
1 teaspoon gherkins, finely chopped

Mix all the ingredients into the mayonnaise.

Fresh Tomato Sauce

1 onion, finely chopped
5 cloves garlic, crushed
4 tablespoons olive oil
1½ lb (700g) ripe tomatoes, roughly chopped
1 tablespoon white sugar
2 tablespoons fruit-flavoured vinegar (raspberry for preference)
1 tablespoon parsley, chopped
1 tablespoon basil, chopped
1 cup water
Salt and pepper

Sauté the onion and garlic in the olive oil until they are golden. Add the rest of the ingredients and simmer gently for 30 minutes at least. Liquidise and pass through a fine sieve. Serve hot or cold, as required.

Uncooked Tomato Sauce for all Grills

1 lb (450g) ripe tomatoes
3 dashes Tabasco sauce
1 tablespoon vinegar
Juice 1 plump clove garlic, crushed
Salt and pepper
4 fl oz (110ml) olive oil
2 tablespoons fresh basil, chopped

Liquidise the tomatoes and strain through a fine sieve – throw away the pips etc which remain in the sieve. Add the rest of the ingredients, whisk with a fork and serve with any grill, particularly fish.

Yoghurt Sauce

11 fl oz (300ml) plain natural live yoghurt
3 tablespoons cucumber, peeled and finely chopped
1 tablespoon chives, chopped
½ teaspoon concentrated mint sauce
Juice of ½ lemon
Salt and pepper

Mix together and chill.

FISH

Vans with corrugated sides, low on the ground like snails with wheels, arrive early in the market square. Bright-faced and burly drivers fold down sides, open flaps, pull out shelves, fiddle with hoses and taps and curse as they push open the huge blue *bâches*, magically transforming the vans into stalls. Wives in clean aprons and rubber boots unload boxes of fish. There are fans of shimmering sardines, trays of beige oysters, mountains of black mussels, pink hummocks of shrimps, creaking baskets of live langoustines. Soft crabs scrabble to the insurmountable walls of polystyrene boxes, congers are coiled, a pyramid of lemons (given free with a reasonable purchase) rises from a field of parsley. Jars of fish soup, dark brown and thick, stand like a guard of honour along the sides of the stall. The sun has not yet risen above the church and there is still more fish to unload.

The merchants prepare their stalls with unhurried style, painting pictures in fish and varnishing the finished canvas with crushed ice. One unfolds a picnic table and lays it with sausage, bread, black olives and wine and, the stall set up, they breakfast upon chunks of bread torn from the loaves with slices of pork and garlic sausage, gabbling of horse racing and the price of fish. In loud voices and generous gestures they tease and poke fun at each other. As the sun broaches the church tower, the ice slowly melts and drips into silver pools beneath the laden stalls.

The first customers arrive. Old men who want just a dozen mussels and a conger cutlet shuffle in carpet slippers, basket in hand and baguette under arm, across the square. Immaculate housewives with painted faces, tight jeans and boots haggle and poke the produce like demons. Poor, fat Arab women load kilo upon kilo of anchovies and sardines into their plastic buckets, while their kaftaned husbands stand in the shade, bearing huge bunches of mint, with a live, terrified rabbit tethered to one ankle.

Black-clad widows select with pursed lips just a *'petite tranche de cabillaud, pour moi . . .'* and bare-legged gypsy women crowd round the huge tuna fish which lies like a black torpedo on a makeshift table at the edge of the market.

The sun is high now and the square is wet with melted ice and littered with fish scales and fins. The babble of the market reaches a mellifluous crescendo, children race in and out of the stalls shrieking. Some stalls have already sold out. And in an hour swarthy dark men dressed in shorts and espadrilles will arrive in a brilliant yellow truck and hose the square with powerful jets, and by 3 p.m. it will again be empty save for a cat jealously gnawing at an overlooked fish head.

Bass Flamed with Fennel and Armagnac

Serves 6

1 bass of at least 3 lb (1.4kg), scaled, gutted and cleaned
1 teaspoon sea salt
Pepper
Olive oil
Bundle of dried fennel stalks, as big in volume but not in weight to the size of the fish
2 glasses Armagnac or eau de vie
½ lemon per person

Slash diagonal cuts into both sides of the fish and rub sea salt into the cuts and skin. Liberally grind pepper over and in the fish and then paint with olive oil.

Grill the bass over the fire, turning from time to time for about 20 minutes, depending on the size of the fish.

While the fish is cooking, erect a stand on an oval fireproof tray and stack the fennel stalks underneath it. When the fish is cooked, transfer it to the stand, pour the alcohol over the fish and fennel stalks and ignite. Leave to burn till the stalks have burnt away – this will impart the most superb flavour and is spectacularly dazzling as you transport it in flames to the table.

Bream Baked in Sea Salt

Serves 4

1 bream, cleaned and gutted but not scaled, about 3 lb (1.4kg)
3 lb (1.4kg) coarse sea salt
Large bunch of parsley to fill cavity of bream

For the herb sauce:
6 tablespoons olive oil
Juice of 1 lemon
1 clove garlic, crushed
3 tablespoons mixed fresh herbs, finely chopped – chives, tarragon, chervil, basil and parsley

Stuff the cavity of the fish with the parsley.

Put half the salt into a fireproof dish and place the bream on top of the bed of salt. Completely cover with the remaining salt and place the dish, well surrounded by hot embers, in the fire and allow to cook for about 45 minutes till the salt is very hard.

Prepare the sauce by whisking all the ingredients together.

Once the bream is ready and the salt is hard, tap it with a heavy knife and lift away the pieces which will pull away the skin of the fish — the fish will be moist and delicate. Lift the fillets from the bone and serve with a little of the herb sauce.

Sweet and Sour Bream Kebabs

Serves 4

2 lb (900g) bream fillets, cut into slices 1 ½ in (4cm) square (or any firm-fleshed white fish)
8 very small tomatoes, cut into quarters
16 small onions, halved

For the marinade:
Juice of 2 lemons
1 clove garlic, crushed
2 pinches of salt

For the basting liquid:
4 tablespoons oil
2 tablespoons sherry
½ teaspoon sugar
Salt and pepper

For the sauce:
1 tablespoon parsley, roughly chopped
1 teaspoon chives, chopped
1 small tub plain yoghurt
4 fl oz (110ml) double cream
Juice of ½ lemon
Salt

Place the pieces of fish in the marinade and leave for about 15 minutes.

Thread 8 skewers alternately with fish, tomato and onion. Paint with the basting mixture. Cook the kebabs for 10 minutes, turning them and basting them often.

While the kebabs are cooking, mix the ingredients for the sauce together. Serve with the sauce apart and a bowl of rice.

Cod Fillets with Lemon

This lemon and bacon mixture will liven up the dullest of fish for the grill.

Serves 4

4 fillets of cod (or any white fish)
2 tablespoons olive oil
4 slices bacon, chopped into strips
2 oz (50g) butter
4 tablespoons capers
1 tablespoon parsley, chopped
2 lemons, cut into tiny pieces, skin and all
Salt and pepper

Salt and oil the 4 fillets and grill them for 4 minutes on each side. While they are cooking, oil a small frying pan and fry the bacon strips until they are golden. Once they are a little crunchy add the butter, capers, parsley and the lemons. Once the butter has melted remove from the heat because this sauce must not cook, it must just warm through.

Place the fish on your serving dish and pour the sauce over and serve with new potatoes.

The bay leaf is indispensable in stews and casseroles and it is vital to many marinades. It is also good to throw on the coals since it releases a wonderful aroma which will subtly flavour the dish that you are cooking, especially oily fish such as mackerel.

Whereas you should never salt meat before you cook it, the reverse is true with fish. Always salt it before you put it on the grill and always turn fish frequently, at least 4 times if they are big and at least twice if they are small.

Grill fish whenever possible with their scales on. This forms a kind of envelope around the fish and enables the juice to stay inside. In any event, if you have grilled your fish golden and crunchy as you should, the scales will have burnt away leaving just the crisp skin.

Whenever possible cut a fish through its natural orifices rather than slitting the whole body open. It is a little difficult, but worth it. Always replace the gut with some fresh herbs.

Mackerel Fillets Baked in Foil Envelopes

This recipe can be applied to any filleted fish you like.

Serves 4

4 large mackerel fillets
4 teaspoons butter
Juice of 1 lime
Salt and pepper
4 small bay leaves
4 small sprigs parsley
4 thin lemon slices
1 heaped teaspoon capers
4 tablespoons single cream

Butter four rectangles of tin foil and place a fillet on each one. Brush each fillet with lime juice and sprinkle with salt and pepper. Place a bay leaf, sprig of parsley and a slice of lemon on each one. Divide the capers between the four fillets, fold up the edges of the foil and anoint each fillet with 1 tablespoon of cream. Close the envelopes and place them near the edge of the fire for about 10 minutes.

Open carefully to avoid spilling any juices and munch away.

Grilled Mackerel

Serves 4

4 mackerel, cleaned
1 lemon, squeezed
Salt
4 tablespoons mixed chopped fresh fennel leaves, parsley, thyme and chervil
1 or 2 cloves garlic, finely chopped
4 fl oz (110ml) oil
4 lemon slices

Slash the mackerel on each side with a sharp knife and sprinkle the inside and outside with some of the lemon juice and salt. Stuff the herbs and some of the garlic into the fish.

Mix the remaining garlic, lemon juice and oil together. Grill the fish for at least 5 minutes on each side until tender, basting with the oil and lemon mixture. Serve with a slice of lemon.

Red Mullet Parcels

Serves 6

12 small red mullet, cleaned
12 thin rashers lean bacon
6 bay leaves, halved
Salt and pepper
Aïoli (see page 31)

Season the fish with salt and pepper. Wrap a piece of bacon around each fish and stick it with a cocktail stick. Insert a bay leaf half between the bacon and the fish.

Grill the fish, turning regularly, for about 10 minutes. Remove the bay leaves and the sticks and serve with a bowl of wobbling aïoli, a green salad and crisp fresh bread.

Grilled Sardines, Sprats, Anchovies or any Small Fish

Aficionados do not gut sardines. They dry them carefully, paint them with herb grilling oil (see page 29) and pop them onto a very hot grill for 3-4 minutes each side. You can eat them with your fingers, which when burnt may be dipped into the tumbler of red wine that your neighbour's wife is holding.

Barbecued Squid with Lemon-Garlic Butter

Serves 4-6

3 lb (1.4kg) squid, skinned and cut into rings
2 oz (50g) butter
6 garlic cloves, finely chopped
Juice of 2 lemons

Sauté the garlic in some of the butter until it is lightly browned. Add the rest of the butter and the lemon juice. Let the butter melt and put the sauce to one side.

Thread the squid rings onto skewers and grill for 2-3 minutes until golden brown. Serve hot with lemon-garlic butter.

Fish in general should be undercooked rather than overcooked, though the skin should be crisp. The flesh should separate from the bones easily but without crumbling.

Grilled Swordfish

Serves 6

6 × 6 oz (175g) swordfish steaks
3 cloves garlic, sliced
Sprigs of rosemary
Olive oil
Salt and pepper

Stick the slices of garlic and sprigs of rosemary into the swordfish. Smear the fish with oil and season well with the salt and pepper. Grill for about 15 minutes over a medium fire until tender.

Swordfish in Lettuce Leaves

Serves 4

4 × 8 oz (225g) swordfish steaks
Juice of 1 lemon
4 tablespoons olive oil
2 tablespoons fennel seeds
½ teaspoon salt
2 cloves garlic, finely chopped
2 tablespoons parsley, finely chopped
1 lettuce, leaves separated

Mix the lemon juice, oil, fennel seeds, salt, garlic and parsley. Marinate the fish in the mixture all day or overnight.

Spread the lettuce leaves flat and place the fish steaks on them, with plenty of the marinade. Cover with more lettuce leaves and tie up securely with string.

Grill the fish, preferably in a hinged grilling basket, over very hot coals for at least 10 minutes on each side. During the last moments of cooking throw some dried fennel branches or fennel seeds over the fire.

Fennel has a beautiful flavour of aniseed which goes very well with grilled fish, especially fish with delicate flesh like bass or John Dory. You can use all the fennel, its fronds, its seeds and its dry stalks. The fronds you chop and put into butter or cream; the seeds you put into marinades; the dry stalks are brilliant when flamed with alcohol under a grilled bass, bream or red mullet.

Tuna with Mustard Sauce

Serves 4

4 slices tuna
2 cloves garlic, finely crushed
1 tablespoon oil
Salt and pepper
4 fl oz (110ml) double cream
2 oz (50g) butter
2 tablespoons strong prepared mustard

Rub the crushed garlic into the fish and oil them on both sides. Cook over a gentle fire for about 15 minutes, turning them every 5 minutes or so. Sprinkle with salt during the cooking process.

While the tuna is cooking, heat the cream in a small saucepan and add the butter in small pieces, whisking as you do, which will thicken the cream. Now add the mustard, salt and pepper and continue cooking and whisking over a low heat for another 2-3 minutes.

Grilled Crayfish

Wherever you have this splendid feast it is going to cost a fortune, so you might as well go the whole hog and buy a really wonderful bottle of white wine to drink with it!

Serves 1

1 live crayfish
2 tablespoons oil
3 oz (75g) soft butter
2 shallots, finely chopped
1 tablespoon finely chopped fresh herbs: parsley, chervil and tarragon
Salt
½ teaspoon black peppercorns, finely crushed

For the very best taste of a crayfish, or a lobster for that matter, I am afraid that you have to cut it in half with a large knife straight down its back. By planting the knife firmly through the back of the head it will die instantly. I appreciate that is repugnant to many people and you may choose to buy an already boiled fish – so be it, but the taste won't be the same.

Paint the flesh with oil and grill flesh-side down for 5 minutes. Then turn it back the other way, shell-side down, and grill for a further 20 minutes. During this time, mix the butter with the shallots, herbs, salt and pepper. By now the flesh of the fish will have contracted, leaving a channel between the flesh and the shell. Into this channel spoon the seasoned butter. Once the butter has melted the crayfish is ready to eat.

Prawns Grilled in Sea Salt

You could serve these prawns on fingers of toasted buttered bread. You can cook langoustines or gambas, indeed all kinds of shellfish, in this way but remember – don't overcook them.

Serves 4

24 large prawns, with shells on
2 tablespoons sea salt
Pinch of cayenne pepper
½ teaspoon of oregano, savory, cumin or fennel seeds

If your grill does not incorporate a flat metal surface then you will have to improvise with an iron frying pan which you place on the coals.

Make sure that the grill is very hot and throw on the salt, cayenne and the herbs. Once this mixture begins to erupt, spit and generally boogie all about, pop on the prawns for 2-3 minutes on each side. Taking care not to burn your fingers, eat these delights with the shells on. The shells will be crunchy and salty and quite splendid and of course will make you very thirsty!

Brochettes of Scallops with Bacon

Serves 4

24 large scallops
1 teaspoon oregano
Pepper
24 thin slices unsmoked bacon, rind off
2 oz (50g) butter
Juice of 1 lemon

Have your fishmonger remove the scallops from their shells if you don't fancy the task. Sprinkle them with oregano and pepper and wrap them carefully in bacon. Thread onto 4 skewers.

Place a drip tray under the grill to catch the juices and grill the brochettes, turning frequently, till the bacon is lightly crisped.

Serve the scallops, which should be firm but slightly undercooked and moist, with the juices from the drip tray which you have whisked together with the butter and the lemon juice and then poured over.

Shellfish and Grape Kebabs

Naturally you can use any combination of fish or shellfish to make this extremely simple and delightful kebab. The important thing is that the fish should be very fresh.

Serves 4

12 langoustine tails
12 large peeled prawns
12 large mussels, cooked and shelled
Large cucumber, cut into ½ in (1cm) thick slices
4 oz (110g) black grapes, de-seeded
4 oz (110g) white grapes, de-seeded
Oil

Thread the ingredients onto 8 skewers in an attractive combination, brush with the oil and grill for about 4 minutes on each side.

Grilled Mixed Fish

If you bought really fresh fish and a good variety, and if you can be bothered to make some good mayonnaise, tartare or aïoli, and you find yourself in the company of a couple of friends and several litres of iced rosé and some good fresh bread – well, all you will need is the sun to shine!

Serves 4

3 lb (1.4kg) of equally sized fish e.g. red mullet, small bream, large sardines, small soles
4 fl oz (110ml) olive oil
2 lemons and the juice of 1 lemon
Salt and pepper
1 teaspoon herbes de Provence
½ Lemon per person

Get your spouse to gut, trim and clean the fish. Then wash and dry them. Marinate the fish in the olive oil, juice of 1 lemon, the salt, pepper and herbs. Turn them from time to time and leave them for about 1 hour.

Pop them onto the grill for 10-15 minutes, depending on their size, basting them with the remainder of the marinade and turning them occasionally. Serve with halves of lemon.

Whole Fish on the Spit

Serves 6

1 × 3 lb (1.4kg) fish (cod, saithe or bream), cleaned with head and tail removed
½ teaspoon paprika
4 tablespoons coriander
6 cardamom pods
1 tablespoon aniseeds or dill
2 onions, chopped
2 cloves garlic, crushed
2 tablespoons mint, chopped
4 tablespoons parsley, chopped
1 green pepper, sliced
5 fl oz (150ml) yoghurt, whipped
Juice of 1 lemon or lime
Salt and pepper
2 oz (50g) ghee (unclarified butter)

Roast the paprika and coriander in a frying pan. Then grind together with the other spices, onions, garlic, herbs and green pepper. Make a paste of this mixture with the yoghurt and lemon juice.

Prick the fish all over and rub the mixture all over it. Season with salt and pepper. Leave to marinate for 1 hour.

Put the fish on the grill with a drip tray underneath to catch the juices. Cook for about 15 minutes until the paste is dry. Baste with the juices from the pan and raise the grill and cook for a further 25 minutes over a more gentle heat until tender. Turn once during the cooking process.

When the flesh flakes easily, the fish is cooked. Now lower the grill to raise the intensity of the heat, baste the fish with the ghee and cook until the skin is crisp. Serve at once.

Unidentified Fish Parcels

A simple and delicious way to cook any white fish is to pop a fillet (one for each parcel) onto a piece of double-thickness buttered foil and season well. For eight servings, divide 4 oz (110g) each of chopped onions and mushrooms, 1 oz (25g) capers, 2 oz (50g) butter, ½ pint (275ml) single cream between each portion. Wrap the foil loosely to make parcels and cook for 25-30 minutes. Serve with chopped parsley and the juices from the fish.

MEAT

Huge purple and cream carcasses hang high in the window from great meat hooks. Below, the white marble shelf is like a painter's palette with freshly squeezed blobs of oil paint: vermilion steaks, pink cutlets, burnt sienna calf's liver, maroon oxtails, ochre eggs piled high, brilliant white lard and sprigs of green parsley. A fine picture indeed – and you can eat it too!

Red-faced butchers saw, chop and fillet, knives flashing over the scrubbed wood tables, while pale apprentices struggle with whole pigs on their shoulders. I draw patterns in the sawdust with the polished toe of my shoe, waiting for a leg of lamb. I'm in no hurry, I love butchers' shops. With such a dazzling choice of meats available it's sad that, for some, barbecuing stops at hamburgers and bangers. Why, with good shopping, careful preparation and planning – essential ingredients for *all* good cooking – you can feast like a Viking warrior off a succulent roast pig, dine on sweet lamb delicately perfumed with rosemary, gorge like a sheikh on kebabs exotically spiced and marinated in yoghurt, or simply sink your teeth into a tender grilled steak.

My leg of lamb has white fat like clotted cream. I prick it with the tip of a small knife and push slivers of garlic and pieces of anchovy fillet into the incisions and squeeze the fat closed so they won't fall out during the cooking process. Finally I push it tightly onto the spit and pour a pastis while the fire settles down, and munch an olive, on this summer day.

The meat is turning golden, beads of condensation run down the bottles of iced rosé, and a silly bee tries to eat the olives as I sit sipping and basting, waiting for my guests who, I hope, will bring a creamy gâteau for dessert. Cool leaves of lettuce in my fingers, as I pour olive oil like yellow Chartreuse into the *saladière* . A grind of coarse salt, a clove of crushed garlic and two chopped anchovy fillets into this salad make it really fine.

The sun is warm and I lay the table with wooden-handled French pocket knives and bulbous glasses. A thrush is busy cracking a snail on a stone anvil under the apple tree, quite oblivious of me. I can hear the lamb sizzling as I daydream – it doesn't matter if you are in Pinner or Provence, a lunch like this knows no boundaries. My friends arrive, noisy and hungry, clamouring for a drink and demolishing the olives in seconds. I carve the lamb, pink slices trimmed with crisp fat. And we eat. Bread and salad. Rosé. Goat's cheese and heavy Côtes du Rhône. Gâteau and Muscat de Beaumes-de-Venise. Dunking sugar lumps into marc and sipping coffee. People are talking at me. But I can't hear a word they are saying.

Daube

Unless you happen to live permanently on an Indian reservation or are one of the charcoal burners from *Swallows and Amazons*, there is not a lot of point in cooking this dish outside because it takes several hours and I reckon that the Martinis would have run out long before it was ready, leaving your guests sprawled out in a stupor over your bijou terrace. So this is a hearth dish. A winter dish. You can sit around the glowing embers sipping mulled wine while a gentle vapour whispers through the ill-fitting lid of the ancient marmite that sits snug against the chimney breast and the odours of beef and wine and wood float deliciously around.

Serves at least 4

2 lb (900g) shin of beef cut into thick slices about 3 in (7.5cm) square
4 oz (110g) chopped fat and lean bacon
3 onions, each stuck with 1 clove
2 small carrots, cut into finger-sized pieces
1 calf's foot
2 tomatoes, cut into quarters
2 shallots
1 tablespoon lard
Salt and pepper
2 bay leaves
1 sprig thyme
2 cloves garlic, crushed
1 sprig of celery head
1 tablespoon parsley, chopped
1 sprig of rosemary
Zest of ½ orange
1 pint (570ml) strong red wine

For the first stage you can use the hob in the kitchen. Melt the lard and olive oil in a large pan. Add the bacon and let it fry for a while. Then add the meat, season with salt and pepper and let it brown a little.

Transfer the meat and bacon to your earthenware cooking pot and keep the fat in the frying pan. Add all the other ingredients, except the orange zest and wine, and fry gently for 5 minutes or till they are all well coated in oil and have just started to colour. Then tip the lot over the beef.

Add the orange zest and red wine and place the pot at the back and to the side of the log fire and go about your business. I suggest that you start cooking the dish in the early afternoon for eating at, say, 8 p.m.

NB Do try and take the trouble to order a calf's foot from your butcher – it enriches the dish beyond compare.

Spit-Roasted Fillet of Beef with Cream and Pepper

Serves 4

2 lb (900g) fillet of beef
2 tablespoons black peppercorns, crushed
3 tablespoons oil
Salt
5 fl oz (150ml) double cream
2 tablespoons Cognac

Roll the joint in the crushed peppercorns until all have been firmly lodged into the meat. Paint with some of the oil and sprinkle with salt.

Place a drip tray under the spit to catch the juices and pop the fillet onto the spit. Cook for about 20 minutes.

Just before the meat is cooked, add the cream to the tray under the meat. Pour the Cognac over the meat and let it flame. Remove the meat to a carving tray or board and leave it to rest for a few minutes. Meanwhile whisk the cream and the juices with a fork, reheat if necessary and pour over the fillet.

Spit-Roast Beef with Paprika

Serves 4

1 piece topside of about 1½ lb (700g)
9 thin slices rolled belly of pork or fatty bacon
1 tablespoon pepper
2 tablespoons paprika
½ teaspoon salt
Glass of eau de vie or brandy
Butcher's string

Cut the beef into 8 slices and cover both the beef and the belly of pork with the salt, pepper and paprika and leave to marinate for at least 1 hour.

Starting with a disc of the pork, thread the two meats onto the spit alternately, to recreate a cylinder-shaped joint – if necessary tie the cylinder with string to hold the shape.

Spit roast the joint for about 20 minutes. When cooked, carefully pull the joint off the spit, preserving the shape, and pour over the alcohol and flame it at the table. Serve with a rich and creamy dish of gratin dauphinoise potatoes which will go very well with this flamboyant little feast.

Rib of Beef with Herbs

Serves 4

3 lb (1.4kg) rib of beef
Black pepper
4 tablespoons olive oil
1 small onion, finely chopped
1 teaspoon thyme
1 teaspoon rosemary needles
2 bay leaves, crushed
12 juniper berries
Salt

Mill black pepper over the rib and leave on a plate.

Mix the olive oil, onion, thyme, rosemary and bay leaves together. Spread this olive oil paste over the meat and leave for 1 hour, turning from time to time.

Seal the meat quickly on both sides over the hottest part of the grill and then cook for 10-12 minutes on each side. During this time pop the juniper berries into the fire. This will add a sweet perfume to the meat. Add salt just before serving, which you should do on a wooden board with a groove to retain the juices as you carve.

A well cooked 'grill' should be golden and crunchy on the outside, tender, juicy and warm inside – whether you like it blue, rare or well done. To achieve this perfect state you must seal the meat on all sides as quickly as possible over the hottest part of the fire. It is the sugar in the meat which caramelises and gives the desired golden, crunchy and appetising result. Of course if the meat is thick you simply raise the meat further from the fire to continue the cooking process.

Never salt the meat before cooking because it will release the juices from the meat, thus ruining the caramelisation process so essential to good flavour and causing the meat to toughen and dry out.

Fillet Steak with Blue Cheese

Fillet steak is horrifically expensive so take care with your cooking. But on the principle of 'in for a penny in for a pound', go the whole hog and spoil yourself with a bottle of really good Burgundy, say Gevrey-Chambertin, and take the trouble to lay a grand table – just because you're eating in the garden it doesn't mean that you have to slum it. So best crystal and porcelain and eat drink and be merry. In style.

Serves 4

4 × 8 oz (225g) fillet steaks
4 oz (110g) butter, softened
4 oz (110g) Roquefort or bleu d'Auvergne cheese
1 tablespoon Cognac
Pepper
1 tablespoon oil

Whisk the butter, cheese, Cognac and pepper into a smooth paste.

Brush the steaks with oil and grill for 3-4 minutes each side (if you like them pink) and spread the cheese butter on each piece and serve at once with jacket potatoes and chive butter.

NB. No salt is required for this dish because the cheese is very salty.

Fillet Steak with Horseradish

Serves 4

4 × 6 oz (175g) fillet steaks

For the marinade:
5 tablespoons oil
4 tablespoons Cognac
Juice of ½ lemon
1 head horseradish, freshly grated (or 2 tablespoons horseradish sauce)
1 clove garlic, crushed to a paste
1 onion, finely grated
2 teaspoons tarragon, chervil and basil, mixed together
Salt and pepper

For the garnish:

Heart of 1 lettuce, cut into 4
4 artichoke hearts, pre-cooked or conserved
4 small tomatoes
8 asparagus spears, pre-cooked or conserved
5 fl oz (150ml) hollandaise sauce (see page 35) with a teaspoon of tomato
    purée stirred in

Mix the marinade ingredients together and coat the fillets with it.
Leave in a covered dish for at least 30 minutes, turning the meat
from time to time.

Grill the steaks over a hot fire for 3-4 minutes on each side.
During this time place the artichoke hearts, asparagus and
tomatoes on the edge of the grill to heat through, garnish with
lettuce leaves and coat with the pink hollandaise sauce.

Fillet Steak with Rum and Bananas

For this recipe you should make some rum punch, hire a steel
band and get your guests limboing under the raspberry canes
while you attend to the food.

Serves 4

4 × 6 oz (175g) fillet steaks
2 cloves garlic
3 tablespoons oil
3 tablespoons dark rum
Pepper
4 bananas, cut in two lengthways
Salt

Peel and then crush the garlic into a paste and mix it with the oil,
the rum and plenty of milled black pepper. Paint this marinade
over the meat and leave for an hour, turning occasionally.

Cook the steaks for 3 minutes on each side. Just before they
are ready, grill the bananas over very hot coals till they start to
char a little. Arrange the meat and bananas on a hot serving
dish, sprinkle with salt and eat.

Never prick meat while it is cooking, or you will lose valuable and
delicious juices. Learn to judge its 'cookedness' by pressing it with your
fingers.

Fillet Steak with Shallot Butter

Serves 4

4 × 6 oz (175g) fillet steaks
2 oz (50g) soft butter
2 shallots, very finely chopped
Salt and pepper

Flatten the fillets with the ball of your hand. Mix the butter and shallots into a paste. Liberally mill black pepper over the steaks and then spread each side with the shallot butter.

Grill the steaks over the fire for 4 minutes each side and serve with fresh green beans, watercress and chips.

Sirloin with Mustard

We all know that some king was supposed to have been so pleased with his Sunday roast that he 'knighted' it (presumably after the post-prandials) and said, 'Arise Sir Loin'. Well, if he had eaten the bit I was offered the other day he'd have called for the butcher and had him beheaded. Sirloin is so expensive that you must buy from a butcher who hangs his meat till it is mature, and if by chance you are sold sub-standard meat take it back and complain like billy-ho.

Serves 4

2 sirloins of about 1 lb (450g) each
1 tablespoon prepared mustard
4 tablespoons oil
Salt and pepper
4 slices smoked bacon
4 tomatoes

Whisk the mustard, oil, salt and pepper together and marinate the steaks for at least 30 minutes. Place a drip tray under the grill to collect the juices and cook the steaks for 5-8 minutes, turning frequently and applying the rest of the marinade as they cook. Just before the steaks are ready grill the tomatoes and bacon.

Cut the steaks into 4, pour any juices from the drip tray over the steaks and accompany with the grilled tomatoes and bacon.

Always cut incisions into the fat of chops and steaks etc. This prevents the grease swamping the meat and hindering the cooking process.

Sirloin Steak with Wine Butter

Serves 4

4 × 8 oz (225g) sirloin steaks
3 oz (75g) wine butter (see page 29)
1 tablespoon nut oil
Salt and pepper

Grind pepper over each steak and rub them well with the oil.
Cook them for 3-4 minutes on each side over a hot fire. Place
them on a hot serving dish, add salt and a slice of wine butter to
each steak.

Minute Steak with Anchovies

Serves 4

4 large, thin slices of sirloin about 6 oz (175g) each
8 salted anchovies (not in olive oil)
4 tablespoons olive oil
4 oz (110g) green olives, pitted
Pepper (no salt because the anchovies are salty)

These are called minute steaks because they cook quickly. They
only cook quickly because they are very thin. Get it?

So oil your meat on both sides, season with pepper, cook on
a hot fire for 2 minutes each side. Then pop two anchovy fillets on
each one, garnish with the green olives and the remainder of the
olive oil. Decorate with sprigs of fresh watercress and serve with
matchstick or game chips.

Beef should ideally be served blue or rare; lamb, kidneys and liver
should be medium and pink; pork and veal should be well cooked.

A well-sealed grill does not mean charred and burnt! So take care that
your fire is stabilised before you begin to cook. Flames and smoke
must not lick around the meat.

It matters not whether you are cooking over wood, charcoal, a picnic
stove or your hearth – always ensure that your chosen apparatus is
hot, well in advance of cooking.

Marinated Steak

Here is another dish for inexperienced husband-cooks. This recipe is ideally suited to the cheaper cuts of beef so it won't matter terribly if he overcooks it. The main thing with husbands is to encourage them as much as possible without risking the housekeeping or your stomach lining.

Serves 4

4 slices of beef steak, about 6 oz (175g) each
1-2 tablespoons cream

For the marinade:
4 tablespoons oil
2 tablespoons wine vinegar
2 tablespoons tomato ketchup
1 tablespoon Worcester sauce
4-5 dashes of Tabasco sauce
1 teaspoon mustard
2 onions, finely chopped
1 clove garlic, crushed

Mix the marinade ingredients together and steep the meat in it for 1 hour.

Grill the meat, turning and basting with the marinade for 6-8 minutes. Any marinade left over can be gently heated with a tablespoon or two of cream and poured over the meat as a sauce.

The Gastronaut's Hamburger

A good hamburger should taste like the sound of 'Under the Boardwalk', a great Rolling Stones song of the late sixties. Anyone found using frozen hamburgers will lose the status of Honorary Gastronaut that comes free with this book.

Serves 4

1½ lb (700g) beef, finely chopped rather than minced
1 hard-boiled egg, finely chopped
1 onion, finely chopped
1 tablespoon chives, parsley and chervil, finely chopped
2 tablespoons olive oil
Salt and pepper
1 tablespoon mild French mustard
Barbecue sauce (see page 31)

Put all the ingredients, except for the barbecue sauce and the mustard, into a bowl and mix very thoroughly and roll into a ball. Now divide the ball into four smaller ones of equal size and with the palm of your hand flatten them to the desired thickness.

Before placing the hamburgers on the grill, spread each one with the mustard. Cook over a very hot fire for 10 minutes, turning them frequently. Serve with the barbecue sauce.

Cheese Hamburgers

Serves 4

1¼ lb (550g) beef, finely chopped
1 large egg
2 oz (50g) Gruyère cheese, grated
2 tablespoons parsley, chopped
1 large onion, finely chopped
½ teaspoon Tabasco sauce
2 tablespoons olive oil
Salt and pepper

Put all the ingredients into a bowl and mix very thoroughly and roll into a ball. Divide the ball into four smaller balls of equal size and with the palm of your hand, flatten them to the desired thickness.

Cook the hamburgers over a very hot fire for 10 minutes, turning them frequently. And instead of chips, make a crispy salad of frisée (curly endive) and radicchio with garlic-flavoured croûtons.

Cumin seeds, whether crushed, whole or powdered, are great, especially with grilled fish like tuna or mackerel, or with meat like lamb and beef.

Herbs are delectable and indispensable flavourings for grills. Use them as you will, singly or mixed, but always with discretion. They should support, refine and augment the taste of the principal ingredient, not dominate or mask it.

Dried herbs are superb in marinades or scattered over the fire during the cooking process. Fresh herbs are best used to enhance sauces, butters, oils etc.

Beef Ball Kebabs

You can have such fun running your fingers through the beef mixture. Quite simple too! Just the job for the old man to do while you sip a Tequila Sunrise, admiring the sunset over your manicured lawns.

Serves 4

1 ¼ lb (550g) ground beef
16 green olives, chopped
1 hard-boiled egg, chopped
5 oz (75g) grated Purmesan cheese
1 small whole lemon, finely minced (take out pips first)
Salt, pepper and nutmeg
2 tablespoons oil, for basting
4 lemon quarters for seasoning the finished dish

Mix the beef, olives, egg, cheese, lemon and seasoning with your fingers till they are well amalgamated and roll them into small balls about 1 in (2.5cm) in diameter. Thread onto skewers and grill for about 10 minutes, basting with oil from time to time. Serve with the lemon quarters and rice.

Spit-Roast Leg of Lamb

1 boned leg of lamb
½ onion, finely chopped
1 clove garlic, finely chopped
Salt and pepper
1 teaspoon thyme or rosemary
1 teaspoon paprika
2 tablespoons oil
4 fl oz (110ml) red wine
1 small tub plain yoghurt
1 tablespoon fresh parsley, tarragon and mint, finely chopped

Mix the onion, garlic, salt, pepper, thyme and paprika together and rub well into the leg of lamb.

Before you put the lamb on the spit remember to place a drip tray underneath it. At this stage it's a good idea to check that the jugs of sangria and kir are well topped up, because you are going to be spending the next hour basting the lamb with oil and this is, I assure you, very thirsty work!

Just before the lamb is cooked, pour the wine over it, making sure that it runs into the drip tray. Now remove the drip tray with all the roasting juices in it, add the yoghurt and the tablespoon of fresh herbs and heat gently, whisking all the time until you have a smooth sauce. And since your garden is probably full of delicious fresh vegetables, why not serve a mixture of runner beans, peas, carrots etc, all lightly cooked and mixed together with butter and freshly-chopped mint?

Spit-Roast Leg of Lamb with Vegetables

Serves 4

1 boned leg of lamb
6 cloves garlic, peeled and sliced like thick almond flakes
1 small tin anchovy fillets
Black pepper
Oil
Large bunch of fresh rosemary twigs
1 tablespoon sea salt

For the vegetable garnish:

8 potatoes, parboiled and cut into pieces 2 in (5cm) in diameter
8 carrots, parboiled and cut into pieces 2 in by 1 in (5cm by 2.5cm)
8 onions, parboiled and cut into pieces 2 in (5cm) in diameter
16 batons celery, parboiled and 2 in (5cm) long
16 whole cloves garlic, unpeeled

Make small incisions all over the leg and insert the slivers of garlic and strips of anchovy deep into the meat. Rub well with black pepper and thread onto your spit.

Place a drip tray under the spit and cook the lamb close to the fire for the first 15 minutes. Then lift higher and baste with oil, cooking for a further hour or so.

About 20 minutes before the end of the cooking process, put all the parboiled vegetables and garlic cloves into the drip tray, which by now has collected fat from the joint – stir the vegetables around to coat them with fat and let them brown and get quite crunchy.

As the cooking process comes to an end and the fire is dying, throw a handful of rosemary onto the fire, having first removed the drip tray, and let it burst into flames. Tip the vegetables and all the juices onto a serving dish, put the leg of lamb on top and leave just at the edge of the fire for 5 or 6 minutes to allow the lamb to 'settle'. Sprinkle the coarse ground sea salt over the lot, carve and serve.

Lamb Chops in Breadcrumbs

Serves 4

4 lamb double loin chops, boned and flattened
5 fl oz (150ml) olive oil
1 garlic clove, crushed
Juice of 1 lemon
2 oz (50g) dry white breadcrumbs
Freshly-chopped parsley

Make a marinade with the oil, garlic and lemon juice and cover the lamb chops. Leave to soak for at least 1 hour.

Before grilling, cover the chops with breadcrumbs. Grill for about 15 minutes, basting with the marinade and turning regularly. Serve sprinkled with the parsley and accompany with ratatouille or onion sauce.

Lamb Chops with Mint

Serves 4

8 lamb chops (or 4 thick slices of leg of lamb)
4 fl oz (110ml) cider vinegar
4 fl oz (110ml) water
1 tablespoon brown sugar
1 tablespoon black peppercorns, finely crushed
Handful fresh mint, finely chopped
1 tablespoon oil
Salt

Bring the cider vinegar and water to the boil. Add the sugar, pepper and the mint. Boil for a further 3 minutes or until the liquid is well reduced.

Now simply oil the chops, seal them quickly for 2 minutes on each side, then using the trusty basting brush paint on the mint sauce. Cook for a further 8-10 minutes depending on your taste, turning occasionally and adding more of the mint sauce. Serve the remaining sauce with the chops.

Before you start to grill make sure that there are no flames and that the cinders are covered in fine white dust. This is when the fire is at its hottest and your meat will seal without scorching, your fat will not run and sausages won't explode.

Lamb Chops with Mushroom Sauce

Serves 4

8 lamb chops
1 oz (25g) butter
4 oz (110g) smoked bacon, very finely chopped
2 medium onions, very finely chopped
5 oz (150g) button mushrooms, finely chopped
4 fl oz (110ml) dry white wine
5 fl oz (150ml) tub of cream
Salt and pepper
1 tablespoon oil

First you must make the sauce. You can do this at any time and heat it through when you want to serve it.

Put the butter, the bacon and the onions into a frying pan and cook for 5 minutes. Then add the mushrooms and pour in the wine. Add salt and pepper to taste and reduce the sauce over a low gas until the wine has almost evaporated. Now add the cream and cook for a further 2 minutes. Pour the sauce into your food processor and liquidise to a smooth creamy sauce – if you are reheating this sauce from cold, do so carefully otherwise it will separate.

Lightly oil the chops and grill them for 3-4 minutes on each side. Sprinkle them with salt and surround with the sauce. Serve with jacket potatoes which you have wrapped in tin foil and cooked in the embers of the fire.

Lamb Chops with Mustard Butter

Serves 4

4 double rib lamb chops, 2 in (5cm) thick
2 tablespoons olive oil
1-2 cloves garlic, crushed
2 tablespoons lemon juice

For the mustard butter:
1 tablespoon French mustard
½ teaspoon lemon juice
1 clove garlic, crushed
4 oz (110g) softened butter
Salt and pepper

Brush the chops with the olive oil, crushed garlic and lemon juice. Season well with salt and pepper and put to one side for a couple of hours.

Mix the mustard, lemon juice and garlic into the softened butter and season well. Keep at room temperature.

Grill the lamb chops for about 7 minutes, depending on how pink you like them. Serve immediately with the butter oozing over the hot chops.

Lamb Chops with Tarragon

Serves 4

4 lamb chops
1 tablespoon tarragon, finely chopped
3 tablespoons olive oil
Salt and pepper
4 tomatoes, cut in half

Mix the tarragon, oil, salt and pepper together and marinate the chops for 2 hours.

Grill the chops and tomatoes for 5 minutes on each side. During the course of the cooking paint on the remainder of the marinade. Once both are cooked, sprinkle with salt and serve with cauliflower cheese.

Lamb Cutlets with Orange Butter

Serves 4

8 lamb cutlets
4 oz (110g) softened butter
2 oranges
1 tablespoon parsley, finely chopped
Salt and pepper

Put ¾ of the butter into a dish with the parsley and a little salt and pepper. Now finely grate the skin of 1 orange and mix into the butter and parsley. Use the juice of this orange to marinate the chops for 1 hour.

Butter the chops with the remaining butter and cook for 4 minutes on each side. Pop a knob of orange butter on each chop and continue cooking till the butter threatens to float off – serve before it does! Accompany with matchstick chips and iced rosé.

Grilled Sardines (page 45) with Grilled Goats' Cheese (page 115)

Marinated Grilled Lamb Kebabs

Serves 6-8

▪ 1½-2 lb (700-900g) leg of lamb or boned lean shoulder

For the marinade:
Juice of 1 lemon
2 cloves garlic, crushed
1 onion, finely grated
1 teaspoon dried oregano
3 tablespoons olive oil
Salt and pepper

Trim the fat off the lamb and cut into 1 in (2.5cm) cubes and put into a bowl. Mix the marinade ingredients and pour over the meat and ensure that all pieces are coated. Leave for at least 1 hour.

Thread the meat onto skewers and cook for 7-10 minutes (more if you like them well done). Turn the skewers frequently, basting with the marinade. Serve with rice and warm pitta bread.

Lamb and Olive Kebabs

Serves 4

1½ lb (700g) shoulder of lamb, cut into 16 equal pieces
16 green olives, stoned (try the big Spanish ones)
2 tomatoes, cut into quarters
1 red pepper, de-pithed, de-seeded and cut into squares
4 slices of smoked bacon, cut in squares
2 tablespoons of oil
Salt and pepper

Thread the ingredients onto the skewers, appropriately apportioned, and grill for 10 minutes, turning from time to time.

Previous left-hand page Daube (page 53)
Previous right-hand page Spit-Roast Leg of Lamb with Vegetables (page 63)
Facing page Ox Heart Brochettes (page 91)

Lamb Kebabs with Yoghurt and Cream

Serves 4

- 1½ lb (700g) lamb, cubed

For the marinade:

- 1 small tub plain yoghurt
- 4 tablespoons double cream
- 3 onions, finely chopped
- 2 cloves garlic, finely crushed
- 1 teaspoon black peppercorns, finely crushed

For the sauce:

- 1 onion, grated
- Juice of 1 lemon
- 5 fl oz (150ml) olive oil

Marinate the cubes of lamb for 2 hours at least.

Thread the meat onto skewers and cook for 10 minutes, turning frequently.

Whisk the ingredients of the sauce together until it emulsifies and serve these delicately flavoured kebabs with rice.

As with sage, you can dry mint and use it when fresh mint is not available. But fresh mint, finely chopped, is exquisite with lamb kebabs and koftas or in Moroccan dishes of beef.

Fresh or powdered ginger is magnificent in marinades for lamb, chicken and pork.

Fresh coriander makes a splendid change from parsley, especially over lamb and pork kebabs. The coriander seeds, quite different in taste from the leaves, are great with grilled fish and dishes of a spicy nature.

Thyme is one of the most useful of herbs. It goes well with almost everything, but it must be used discreetly. And don't forget that it is stronger dried than fresh. Mixed with bay leaves, savory, nutmeg and lavender it becomes that delicious mixture known as 'Herbes de Provence'.

Indian Minced Lamb Kebabs

All the following spicy lamb dishes are perfect with mint tea, hot or iced, but because your guests will think you mean if you do not offer them alcohol, why not lace the tea with crème de menthe and vodka? And soon they will be singing desert songs.

Serves 6

2 lb (900g) lamb or mutton, minced twice and worked to a paste with hands or food processor
2 teaspoons each of ground cinnamon, ground mace, ground cloves, ground nutmeg
1 tablespoon roasted and ground coriander seeds
1 teaspoon garam masala
1 teaspoon roasted and ground cumin
1 large onion, grated
3 cardamom pods, husks removed
Small amount of fresh ginger root, crushed
Lemon juice
3 garlic cloves, crushed
3 tablespoons yoghurt
3-4 sprigs of parsley, chopped
3-4 mint leaves, chopped
3-4 sprigs of coriander leaves, chopped
½ green chilli pepper, chopped (or ½ teaspoon cayenne pepper)
Salt and pepper
Olive oil
6 wedges of lemon, to garnish
2 thinly sliced onions for garnish, sprinkled with salt and left to soften for 30 minutes

Mix the meat with all the above ingredients except for the oil, the lemon wedges and the softened onion slices. Leave to stand in a cool place for several hours.

Press the meat into sausage shapes and thread onto round skewers (flat-bladed so that the meat does not slip). Cook over a medium heat for about 20 minutes, turning and basting with olive oil if it looks a little dry. The kebabs should be brown but not overcooked. Serve with the lemon wedges and slices of onion.

> Please don't follow to the letter the times that I give for cooking. Obviously they will vary depending upon the thickness of the meat and the intensity of the coals.

Indian Kebabs

Serves 4

▭ 1 ½ lb (700g) shoulder of lamb, cubed

For the marinade:

5 fl oz (150ml) coconut milk
½ teaspoon dry ginger
½ teaspoon cayenne pepper
½ teaspoon powdered cumin
1 teaspoon sugar
Salt and pepper

For the sauce:

4 oz (110g) peanuts or pistachios, diced
5 fl oz (150ml) coconut milk
2 tablespoons oil
Juice of ½ lemon
1 small onion, finely chopped
1 clove garlic, finely chopped
1 teaspoon vinegar
1 teaspoon sugar
Salt and pepper

Add the diced lamb to the marinade and leave for 1 hour.

While the lamb is marinating make the sauce by whacking all the ingredients into the merry food processor and whizzing at maximum speed for 2 minutes until beautifully smooth. Pour into a sauceboat and leave in the fridge.

Thread the lamb onto skewers and grill them, turning frequently for about 10 minutes.

And wouldn't it be terrific to wander down to the very bottom of the garden, gather huge sprigs of fresh mint and make some delicious iced mint tea. Follow these simple instructions and all the juices of the Orient will be yours!

The flavour of rosemary is very strong but it goes well with beef, pork, lamb, veal, chicken and some fish, particularly oily ones such as red mullet, anchovies and sardines. The best rosemary is to be found on the roadsides of Provence where the hot sun pumps it full of flavour.

Moroccan Kebabs

Serves 4

1¼ lb (550g) minced lamb or beef
½ teaspoon cinnamon
1 teaspoon powdered cumin
2 teaspoons paprika
Pinch of cayenne pepper
2 tablespoons parsley, finely chopped
1 tablespoon fresh coriander, finely chopped
1 large onion, finely grated
12 large leaves of fresh mint
2 tablespoons oil
Salt

Keep aside the mint leaves, oil and salt, but mix everything else by hand into 12 balls.

Put each ball onto a skewer and squeeze it out until you have a sausage shape about 2½ in (6cm). Wrap each sausage with a fresh mint leaf. You must take care to pinch the sausage on tightly so that it does not fall off in the cooking process.

Paint with oil and grill for 6-8 minutes, turning frequently. Add salt just before serving.

Oriental Lamb Kebabs

Serves 4

1¼ lb (550g) shoulder of lamb, cut into cubes
16 small onions, cut in half
Salt and pepper

For the marinade:
4 fl oz (110ml) oil
½ teaspoon cinnamon
½ teaspoon cumin
Pinch of cayenne pepper

Marinate the meat for at least 2 hours in the oil, cinnamon, cumin and cayenne.

Skewer the meat and the onions alternately and grill for 15 minutes, turning frequently. Season with salt and pepper and serve with cucumber dressed with yoghurt and lemon juice.

Grilled Spiced Minced Lamb Balls

Serves 4

1¼ lb (550g) shoulder of lamb, minced
1½ oz (40g) sultanas
½ tablespoon curry powder
Salt and pepper
4 oz (110g) caul
3 medium onions, cut into ¼ in (0.5cm) thick slices
1 tablespoon oil

Mix the lamb, sultanas, curry powder, salt and pepper together and form into balls about 1½ in (4cm) in diameter. Wrap each one carefully with a piece of caul. Thread onto skewers with a disc of onion between each one.

Brush the meat balls and onion with oil and cook for about 10 minutes, turning frequently. Serve with some rice, garnished with sultanas, toasted flaked almonds and quarters of hard-boiled egg.

Another Lamb Kebab

Serves 4

1½ lb (700g) lean lamb, cubed
Salt and pepper
5 fl oz (150ml) soy sauce
Juice of ½ lemon
2 cloves garlic, crushed
2 onions, sliced for garnish

Season the meat with salt and pepper and marinate in a mixture of the soy sauce, lemon juice and garlic for about an hour.

Thread the meat onto skewers and grill for about 15 minutes, turning regularly. Serve with sprinklings of soy sauce and garnish with the sliced raw onion.

Make sure that whatever food you are cooking is taken out of the fridge at least one hour before you plan to cook.

When grilling more than one chop or steak ensure that they are cut to a uniform size so that they cook evenly and together. Similarly when cutting meat or vegetables for kebabs.

Sheftalia

What better excuse for gallons of resiny Greek wine, loud music and dancing could you have than this delicious dish? A number of supermarkets sell those lovely honey-filled shredded wheat Greek desserts, so buy a few for pud.

Serves 4

9 oz (250g) lamb, minced
9 oz (250g) pork, minced
1 large onion, finely chopped
1 teaspoon oregano, finely chopped
2 tablespoons parsley, finely chopped
Salt and pepper
4 oz (110g) lamb's caul, rinsed and cut into 12 pieces
Lemon wedges for garnish

Mix the meats, onion and herbs together. Season well with salt and pepper. Shape the meat into 12 plump sausages and wrap each one in a piece of the lamb's caul.

Grill for 8-10 minutes, turning frequently. Serve with rice, salad and lemon wedges.

Suckling Pig stuffed with Herbs

This crispy, crackly feast will cause you all sorts of trouble if you are not patient. Make sure that your fire is well maintained, the beast frequently turned and basted and that you cook it for long enough — which in the event is bound to be longer than you or the recipe thinks! I should lay on a barrel of cider or beer for the cook, and let the guests drink what's left.

A Feast for 12

1 suckling pig, about 12 lb (5.4kg), ordered from your butcher well in advance

For the stuffing:

1 bunch of thyme
1 bunch of parsley
1 bunch of rosemary
12 bay leaves
1 tablespoon dried fennel
1 tablespoon crushed peppercorns
1 tablespoon sea salt
10 cloves garlic, crushed but not peeled

Basting mixture:

- 4 fl oz (110ml) olive oil
- 4 fl oz (110ml) dry white wine
- 3 cloves garlic, finely chopped
- 1 teaspoon salt

Rub salt and pepper inside the pig and stuff it with all the herbs. Sew up the opening securely so that nothing falls out during the cooking process.

This little pig is going to take about 2½ hours to cook on the spit so don't have it too close to the fire to start with or it will burn before it cooks through. Do not baste the pig until it has been cooking for at least 30 minutes – by the way, the purists would paint the basting mixture on with a sprig of fresh rosemary, but it's OK to use your normal basting brush. Remove the herb stuffing before serving.

Spit-Roast Loin of Pork

Serves 4

- 2 lb (900g) boned and rolled loin of pork with rind off
- 6 cloves

For the basting mixture:

- 1 tablespoon prepared mustard
- 3 tablespoons oil
- Juice of 1 lemon
- 4 fl oz (110ml) soy sauce
- Salt and pepper
- 2 cloves garlic, crushed

Spike the meat with the cloves and put it onto the spit and secure well.

Mix all the basting ingredients together in a bowl and paint the joint. Cook for about 1 hour, basting all the while. Serve with a purée of celeriac.

> Fresh basil is a fabulous herb. Freshly chopped over cooked meat it is excellent, or indeed crushed with garlic, salt, olive oil and poured over grilled chicken, lamb or fish – especially prawns, crayfish and scallops. Never use dried or powdered basil – OK, it smells of eau de Cologne, but do you really want your food to taste of aftershave? Just buy a plant and grow it on the window ledge.

Roast Loin of Pork

Serves 6-8

4 lb (1.8kg) loin of pork
1 sprig of fresh rosemary, leaves finely chopped
2 cloves garlic, finely chopped
Salt and pepper

Mix the chopped rosemary and garlic with a teaspoon of salt and lots of pepper.

Make holes in the meat with a small sharp knife – getting as close as possible to the bone. Put some of the rosemary and garlic mix into the holes and season the meat well.

Skewer the meat securely onto the spit and cook for at least 2 hours, turning regularly, until the juices run clear when the meat is pierced. Carve and serve hot or cold.

With sage in the garden, so the proverb says, one has no need of a doctor. This splendid herb, which is as good dried as it is fresh, is particularly good with fish, vegetables and pork.

A well-butchered pig leaves nothing but the grunt, so they say. I love pork. In Portugal the chops are milky white and juicy. Charcoal grilled, and sprinkled with sea salt served with a salad of green tomatoes, onion rings and crunchy lettuce hearts tossed in olive oil, they are a feast for anyone. And roast leg of Old Spot with thick fat and crackling that melts in the mouth with sage and onion stuffing and apple sauce is second to none. In Provence a roast pig's head is highly esteemed and quite delicious. You score it like a normal joint of pork, salt it well and roast for hours and hours in the oven. The tongue and brains are delicious bonuses. Spanish immigrants in France have a particular love of pigs' ears. They grill them till they are crisp like popadoms and then nibble at them while sipping the evening apéritif on the porch. I've tried them and they are brilliant – they leave pork scratchings for dead. But back to the barbecue department. When you see some fresh green and red chillis in the shops, buy enough to half-fill a Kilner jar (buy one if you don't already possess one), add some pickling spice and real malt vinegar and pickle the chillis just as you would onions. Then when you decide to make some simple pork kebabs and can't be bothered with sauces or marinades just nibble a little of the chilli with each mouthful. Very hot but superb.

Marinated Pork with Chillies

Serves 4

1½ lb (700g) pork cut into thin 4 in (10cm) pieces
4 fresh chillies
2 dried chillies
2 small onions
Piece of fresh ginger root
½ oz (10g) tamarind
1 tablespoon soft brown sugar
Pinch of saffron
12 fl oz (350ml) coconut milk
Salt

Crush the fresh and dried chillies, onions, ginger root and tamarind to a paste. Add the sugar, saffron and the coconut milk.

Season the pieces of pork with salt and marinate the meat in the spice and coconut mixture for about 2 hours, turning frequently.

Grill the pork pieces, basting them frequently with the marinade, for 3-4 minutes each side. Heat the remaining marinade and pour it over the cooked meat.

Pork Chops with Fennel

Serves 4

4 pork chops
Pepper
2 oz (50g) soft butter
2 tablespoons fennel seeds
Salt

Grind masses of pepper over the chops and butter them both sides. Grill for 10-12 minutes, turning a couple of times and basting with butter.

Just before the chops are cooked, sprinkle the fennel seeds over them and let some fall into the fire – this will heighten the aromatic effect of the fennel. Simple but very delicious. Accompany with a salad of thinly sliced raw fennel bulbs seasoned with olive oil, salt and lemon juice.

Pork Kebabs with Green Peppercorns

Serves 4

1¼ lb (550g) pork, cut into 1 in (2.5cm) cubes
6 oz (175g) smoked bacon, cut into small cubes
2 tablespoons Cognac
1 tablespoon green peppercorns
Salt

Crush the peppercorns into a paste and mix in the Cognac. Stir in the pork and bacon pieces and leave to marinate for at least 2 hours.

Thread onto skewers and cook for about 12 minutes, turning and basting frequently. Season with salt and serve with rice.

Pork Kebabs with Pineapple

Serves 4

1½ lb (700g) fillet of pork, cut in slices 1 in (2.5cm) thick
8 cocktail sausages
8 pieces of canned pineapple soaked in white rum
8 prunes soaked in red wine for 3-4 hours
3 tablespoons oil
1 teaspoon prepared mustard
1 teaspoon paprika
Salt

Thread the pork, sausages, pineapple and prunes onto 4 skewers.

Mix the oil, mustard, salt and paprika to a paste and paint it over the kebabs. Grill the kebabs for 15 minutes, with a drip tray containing the rest of the basting paste underneath. Turn the kebabs several times and baste with the mixture from the drip tray.

Serve the kebabs with the marinade and the juices from the meat, which will have amalgamated to make a delicious sauce – add the rum that you macerated the pineapple with to make it stretch further if you like.

Pork and Prune Kebabs

Serves 4

12 oz (350g) fillet of pork, cubed
12 oz (350g) pig's liver
16 prunes, soaked overnight in red wine
3 tablespoons oil
Salt and pepper

Ensure that the meat and liver cubes are roughly the same size as the prunes.

Thread the meat, liver and prunes alternately onto 4 skewers, brush with oil and grill for 10 minutes or so. Season with salt and pepper and serve.

Pork and Sage Kebabs

Serves 4

1 lb (450g) pork fillet, cubed
24 fresh sage leaves
24 button mushrooms
24 cubes bread
Oil
Salt and pepper

Load 4 skewers with the meat, sage, bread and mushrooms in the order of your preference. Paint them with oil and grill gently for about 15 minutes, turning several times. Season with salt and pepper and serve with mashed potato topped with cheese and gratinéed.

Spiced Spare Ribs

Serves 4

3 lb (1.4kg) lean pork spare ribs, trimmed and chined for ease of separating after cooking

For the marinade:
4 tablespoons hoisin sauce
2 oz (50g) sugar
1 tablespoon rice wine or dry sherry
1 tablespoon Chinese oyster sauce
½ teaspoon Chinese five-spice powder

Mix all the ingredients for the marinade together. Cover the spare ribs and leave for at least 4 hours.

Cook over medium hot coals, turning occasionally, for about 30-40 minutes until brown.

Glazed Spare Ribs

Serves 4

1 × 4 lb (1.8kg) strip of spare ribs, trimmed and chined for ease of separating after cooking
3 tablespoons oil
2 onions, finely chopped
1 clove garlic, crushed
½ teaspoon thyme
4 fl oz (110ml) water
4 tablespoons cider vinegar
Juice of ½ lemon
1 tablespoon prepared mustard
2 tablespoons honey
4 tablespoons tomato ketchup
2 tablespoons Worcester sauce
2 pinches of cayenne pepper
1 clove

Heat the oil and gently fry the onion and garlic until transparent. Now add everything else except the spare ribs and cook for a further 10 minutes or so till you have a thick red paint.

Grill the ribs gently for about 40 minutes over a drip tray (serve any juices as sauce), while you apply the basting liquid to them with a paint brush and turn them from time to time. The ribs are ready when they are crunchy and caramelised and have a shiny reddish colour. Serve with a dish of deep-fried onions. Offer bowls of jasmin tea for the guests to wash their fingers in, and let them drink warm sake.

Merguez

These are the most brilliant sausages in the world. Small, hot and spicy, they are truly excellent for an inspired party. Of course, if you live in the South of France or London you just wander into the butcher's or Harrods or some such and buy them. But you can make them yourself.

The first step is to ensure that your food processor has a sausage-stuffing attachment. Pop out and buy some casings from your friendly neighbourhood butcher. Soak these intestinal tubes in warm water and lemon juice to clean for about thirty minutes. Then stuff a funnel into one end and run water through to ensure there are no punctures.

Now you must mince some very fatty pork, belly would be fine. To 1 lb (450g) of the finely minced pork add a teaspoonful of harissa (see page 32), half a teaspoonful of herbes de Provence and salt and pepper. Clip on the sausage-stuffing attachment and fill up the tubes. *Merguez* should be about 3 inches (7.5cm) long, so when you have filled a tube to the limit squeeze a space every 3 inches (7.5cm) and tie a knot in the skin. To cook them, brush with olive oil and grill till well cooked. Black and white sausages (*boudins*) are also superb when grilled and served with a bowl of apple sauce.

Veal and Kidney Kebabs

Serves 4

7 oz (200g) calf's kidney
10 oz (275g) veal fillet
5 oz (150g) fat bacon, thickly sliced and cut into 1 in (2.5cm) squares
2 German sausages (Bratwürst), cut into 1 in (2.5cm) discs
8 small onions, peeled and blanched in boiling water for 5 minutes
1 large red pepper, de-pithed, de-seeded and cut into 1 in (2.5cm) squares
    and blanched in boiling water for 3-4 minutes

For the marinade:
4 tablespoons olive oil
1 tablespoon parsley, chopped
½ teaspoon cayenne pepper
Pinch or two of salt

Remove the skin, core and gristle from the kidneys and cut them and the veal into 1 in (2.5cm) cubes. Now, using all your artistic skill, thread all the ingredients onto 8 skewers, ensuring that the fat bacon is always next to the kidneys.

Steep them well in the marinade for 10 minutes or so before grilling them for 5 minutes on each side.

OFFAL

'Will Scotty get back in time? Or is it too late for . . . Dick Barton – Special Agent? Tune in tomorrow night!' said the announcer.

'What's for supper?' I said. Although I knew the answer.

It was always faggots and peas after Dick Barton on Thursdays. When the van came round I would stand in the rain while the fat man with a thin moustache and stained white coat filled my white pudding basin with faggots and peas, overflowing with thick gravy which I licked on the way down the garden path. And swallowed a hot finger-full of sweet mushy peas before I closed the door.

We ate offal of all kinds in our house. Chitterlings for breakfast, roast stuffed heart for lunch, liver and bacon for supper. Sometimes golden fried sweetbreads with butter and capers, sometimes boiled pigs' trotters, hot and gelatinous, with salt and pepper and vinegar, and on cold winter days tripe in a creamy onion sauce with doorsteps of bread and butter. And breakfasts. Oh, we had good breakfasts. Hogs' puddings with fried laver bread; thick slices of fat bacon with field mushrooms (if my Uncle Ken hadn't sold them first to the Red Lion Hotel!); crisp slices of black pudding marbled with diamonds of pork fat, and grilled tomatoes.

Mealtimes were precise affairs. However delicious mum's own faggots were, you had to eat them before *Hancock's Half Hour* or *The Goon Show*. How could you concentrate on the two finest things in a boy's life at the same time? Especially when – more important than homework – you needed to know every line of Hancock for school the next day.

Some days the kitchen at home resembled an operating theatre from some farcical 'Carry On' film. Clad in a huge apron and head band, the table bloody with spongy pink pigs' lights, a heart, liver, caul, a pig's head balefully peeking from behind a pile of onions, bunches of dried sage falling to the floor, mother would scold me for leaving mud on the floor after I had picked the parsley from the bottom of the winter garden. The windows steamed up as she went to work with a knife and huge pots of steaming stock. During Worker's Playtime we ate bread and pickles in the middle of the surgery. And in the quiet afternoon I dried and offered for inspection a million bowls for brawn. We minced the lights and heart and livers and rolled them in caul. We stirred and thickened, we licked and tasted. And that night I ate 7 wonderful faggots, thickly wrapped with crisp fat caul.

But I don't remember what happened to Dick Barton – Special Agent.

The cooking and preparation of offal for the outdoor grill should be taken as seriously as did my mother in her labours over faggots and brawn. A certain amount of time will have to be spent in the kitchen before your actual performance on the terrace. The following recipes are not, of course, a definitive list, but are really intended to show that there is more to barbecues than meal-filled hamburgers and warm gin. Make some sauces in the calm before the guests arrive, marinate at your leisure, get the old boy peeling the skin from the kidneys or rolling the caul around the liver. Have a drink while you are doing it. This is not an endurance test, it is meant to be fun. And if, at the last moment, it pours with rain carry on with the grill on your stove, electric or gas. It really doesn't matter.

Grilled Pigs' Trotters

The difficulty with this simple and delicious meal is in obtaining cooked pigs' trotters, or calves' feet for that matter, and I think it hardly worth buying 2 pigs' trotters to simmer for hours in preparation for this exquisite little snack. So use a butcher who cooks his own hams etc, and ask him to provide you with a couple of cooked ones for next week.

Serves 4

> 2 pigs' trotters, cooked and boned and cut in half
> 4 tablespoons oil
> Juice of ½ lemon
> 1 teaspoon chopped parsley
> 4 oz (110g) breadcrumbs
> Salt and pepper

Marinate the trotters in the oil, lemon, parsley, salt and pepper for 1 hour. Then dredge the trotters in the breadcrumbs, pressing with your hand to make sure that the breadcrumbs stick. Place them on the grill for 10 minutes each side and occasionally paint them with the remainder of the marinade.

These trotters will provide you with a magnificent excuse to sample one of the little ethnic hand-made pots of mustard that somebody gave you for Christmas!

Grilled Calf's Liver

Serves 4

4 × 4 oz (110g) slices calf's liver, ½ in (1cm) thick
Salt
Pepper
Olive oil
Lemon wedges

Sprinkle salt over the grill rack and when the fire is very hot place each slice on and cook for about 45 seconds each side – the liver should be brown on the outside and a beautiful light pink on the inside. Sprinkle the cooked liver with pepper and olive oil and garnish with wedges of lemon.

Liver and Banana Kebabs

Serves 4

12 very thin slices of calf's liver
Salt and pepper
24 fresh sage leaves
3 green bananas (if not green then not over-ripe)
Juice of 1 lemon
2-3 oz (50-75g) melted butter
Large measure of Cognac
Green piquant sauce (see page 32)

I hope that the mathematics of this excellent dish won't confuse you. First cut the liver slices in half, lay each piece flat and sprinkle with salt and pepper. Then lay a fresh sage leaf on each piece and roll the liver into a tight sausage shape.

Next cut the bananas into 24 discs and thread the liver and banana alternately onto 8 skewers and paint them with the lemon juice (especially the bananas). Now paint them with the melted butter and grill for about 5 minutes, basting with more butter and turning frequently.

Once cooked pop them onto a serving dish, warm the Cognac and pour it over the kebabs and set fire to it. Carry them flaming to the table and I promise you that your guests will go . . . . over this dish.

Chicken Liver Kebabs

Serves 4

1 lb (450g) chicken livers
4 oz (110g) butter
1 onion, finely chopped
1 teaspoon sage, finely chopped
Pinch of grated nutmeg
Salt and pepper
24 very thin slices of smoked bacon

Melt the butter in a pan and fry the onion till transparent. Add the chicken livers for 1-2 minutes, season with sage, salt, pepper and nutmeg. Allow to cool.

Now my little gastronauts, this will be the moment when you regret you did not read the recipe in its entirety before commencing to cook, because you must now wrap each slice of bacon carefully around the chicken livers and thread them gently onto 4 skewers – which is very fiddly. But since you have to cook them for only 2½ minutes or until the bacon crisps a little, you will find your effort will be quickly rewarded with the fine flavour of these little delicacies.

Marinated Liver with Bacon

Serves 4-6

1½ lb (700g) lamb's liver, cut into thick slices
4-6 rashers bacon, rinds removed

For the marinade:
5 tablespoons olive oil
1 lemon, squeezed
1 tablespoon parsley, finely chopped
Salt and pepper

Mix together the marinade ingredients and coat the liver slices in a shallow dish. Leave for 1 hour.

Drain the liver, keeping the marinade to one side. Grill the slices of liver for 10-12 minutes over a medium fire, turning once. Grill the bacon until it is crispy and brown. Heat the marinade and serve with the liver and bacon.

Liver and Apple Kebabs

Serves 4

1 lb (450g) veal or lamb's liver, cut into 1 in (2.5cm) cubes
4 oz (110g) fat bacon, cut into squares to match the liver
8 small onions, halved
2 eating apples, cored but not peeled and cut into quarters
4 tablespoons oil
Pepper
Barbecue sauce (see page 31)

Thread the ingredients onto 4 skewers and paint with oil and sprinkle with pepper.

Grill for about 15 minutes, turning and basting frequently. Serve with grated potatoes, fried in butter till golden but still slightly crunchy, and barbecue sauce.

Liver Kebabs with Cumin

Serves 4

1½ lb (550g) lamb's or calf's liver, cut into 1½ in (4cm) cubes
1 teaspoon powdered cumin
Salt and pepper
6 oz (175g) caul
4 lemon wedges

Powder each piece of liver with cumin, salt and pepper. Cut the caul into squares large enough to envelop the liver cubes completely.

Thread the liver onto 4 skewers and grill for about 8 minutes, turning frequently. Serve with a wedge of lemon and some potatoes sautéed with finely sliced onions.

Chicken Liver Kebabs with Madeira

Serves 4

1 lb (450g) chicken livers
Salt
1 lemon, cut into quarters

For the marinade:
- 4 fl oz (110ml) Madeira
- 4 fl oz (110ml) soy sauce
- 2 onions, finely grated
- Salt and pepper

Mix the marinade ingredients together, and leave the chicken livers in the marinade for at least 1 hour before carefully threading onto 4 skewers.

Grill them for 3-4 minutes, turning frequently until they are slightly crisp on the outside and pink in the middle. Season with salt and serve with quarters of lemon, melted butter and rice.

Ox Heart Brochettes

Throughout Provence in the summer months you will see café terraces crammed with folk merrily munching morsels from thin pieces of wire. A middle-aged man with a tea towel tucked into his Levis to cover his corpulent stomach will be perspiring patiently as he stands before the intense heat of a rusty steel contraption with a crooked chimney bellowing smoke into the purple night. A small boy, his son, will dart sure-footed between the crowded tables answering the hungry call 'Encore une douzaine!', juggling with plates piled high with spindly brochettes.

You will swig rosé as you eat a dozen or so skewers' worth, dipping each piece into a saucer of harissa – a fiercely hot pepper paste from North Africa which gives the little cubes of ox heart a truly exotic flavour.

These delicious brochettes are cheap and easy to prepare and, as with merguez (see page), make the perfect food for a big summer party. In case your friends are a little conservative it might be as well to omit to tell them what the meat really is till after they've eaten it!

You will need:
- Ox heart, cut into ½ in (1cm) cubes
- Large quantity of speck (fat bacon), cut into ½ in (1cm) squares
- Pepper
- Olive oil
- Herbes de Provence
- Harissa (see page 32)

These delicious brochettes are cheap and easy to prepare and, as with merguez (see page 83), make the perfect food for a big summer party. In case your friends are a little conservative it might be as well to omit to tell them what the meat really is till after they've eaten it!

You will need:

Ox heart, cut into ½ in (1 cm) cubes
Large quantity of speck (fat bacon), cut into ½ in (1 cm) squares
Pepper
Olive oil
Herbes de Provence
Harissa (see page 32)

I have not given precise quantities here because I don't know how many people you will be inviting to your party. But the technique is simple and you can prepare them well in advance.

Simply thread a cube of meat, then a square of fat, on each skewer and paint with herbs, pepper and oil which you previously mixed together. Place on the hot grill for about 3-4 minutes, turning at least once. Serve with the hot and spicy harissa sauce.

Calf's Kidneys with Prunes

Serves 4

2 calf's kidneys
2 tablespoons vinegar
16 prunes
16 thin slices smoked bacon
Salt
3 tablespoons French mustard
9 fl oz (250ml) double cream

Halve the kidneys and remove the core of fat. Put the kidneys into a bowl of water, add the vinegar and leave for 5 minutes. Rinse and dry the kidneys with kitchen paper. Cut them into 24 pieces.

Soak the prunes for about 20 minutes in warm water. Remove the stones and wrap each one in a slice of bacon. Then, beginning and ending with a piece of kidney, thread the kidney pieces and prunes onto 8 small skewers.

Cook for about 15 minutes, until well done, on a hot grill. Add salt off the heat and accompany with the sauce you have made by simply mixing the cream and mustard together.

Sweetbreads in Envelopes

Serves 4

1¼ lb (550g) veal sweetbreads
2 oz (50g) melted butter
1 heaped tablespoon finely chopped fresh herbs, to include tarragon, parsley
  and chervil
Salt and pepper
4 large croûtons, fried in butter

Wash the sweetbreads well under cold running water for
10 minutes or so and then plunge them into boiling water for
3 or 4 minutes. Rinse under cold water and dry them. Cut them
into 4 slices, paint them with the melted butter and place each
one into a foil envelope. Wrap the tin foil to make parcels and
cook over the embers of your fire for 5 minutes on each side.

Open the foil parcels, take out the slices of sweetbread and
place them on the grill for a moment or two on each side till they
turn golden. Then place each slice on a croûton, sprinkle with the
mixed herbs, season with salt and pepper and serve with fresh
spinach from your garden.

Sweetbread Kebabs with Madeira Sauce

Serves 4

1 lb (450g) veal sweetbreads
Juice of 1 lemon
6 oz (175g) button mushrooms, of a uniform size
6 oz (175g) piece smoked bacon, cut into rectangles
4 oz (110g) fresh white breadcrumbs
2 oz (50g) melted butter
Salt and pepper
Madeira sauce (see page 36)

Cover the sweetbreads with the lemon juice and salted cold
water for 20 minutes. Then peel off the membrane and any traces
of blood etc. Dry them and cut them into cubes about the same
size as the mushrooms.

Thread the ingredients onto 4 skewers, paint them with melted
butter, roll them in the breadcrumbs and grill gently for about 15
minutes, turning and basting with butter all the while. Season with
salt and pepper and serve with grilled tomatoes and sauté
potatoes. And, of course, the sauce, piping hot in a sauce boat.

POULTRY AND GAME

Winter has come but the sky is still a brilliant blue. The church square, which was so busy, so frenetic and colourful in summer, with its market stalls and the bright parasols of the pavement cafés that were thronged with beautiful people, sipping and smiling, in their bold coloured clothes, is now desolate.

The massive walls of the church are grey and old. A priest, one hand on his beret the other clutching a basket, struggles against the screaming Mistral across the bleak cobbled square to the sanctity of his vestry, his cassock flying like the ripped missen of a crabber in a storm. A cat mews against the tightly shuttered window of the bakery.

I stand with my back to the stove in the bar. Four old men, unshaven under their caps, silently flick cards onto the felt mat. There are no glasses on the table. They won't drink till five. Just play cards.

It is a favourite time of the year for me. The quiet afternoons can last forever as I sip coffee and dip sugar lumps into my marc. Tonight is the Grand Loto here in the Café de France. A noisy drunken night with endless prizes to be won. And argued over. The prizes hang outside in front of the café windows, safe in the freezing afternoon and too sacred for anyone to steal.

A wild boar hangs by its hind legs, flanked by a brace of pheasants and red furred hares. The brilliant emerald green feathers of wild duck glint and flash. A ham, peppered black, sways encrusted in its net. Rabbits next to salamis. Sprout baskets filled with bottles chink as the wind tugs at this delicious tableau.

The shops will re-open soon. The *traiteur's* window is filled with game. Multi-coloured corpses, brilliant in death as in life, sombre fur and fine feather, the speckled brown and cream breasts of thrushes and neatly plucked quails with just a ruff of feather around their necks lie to attention. Partridge and pigeons hang from the chrome rail above them. And the back shelf is piled high with tins of foie gras, truffles and *pâté de grive* (thrush pâté). Signs in the window offer jugged hare, venison stew and crayfish armoricaine '*prêt à emporter*' – ready to take away.

Tonight after the Grand Loto, win or lose, I will eat well with friends who have promised me a rare treat: a *brochette des oiseaux provençals* – thrushes basted with olive oil and garlic and grilled in the embers of the hearth and eaten off croûtons spread with game pâté. Washed down with litres of coarse fruity red wine from Mont Ventoux.

Yes, I like this time of year.

Roast Stuffed Chicken

To my mind the average frozen chicken is tasteless. If you are not lucky enough to have free-range ones pecking about the bottom of the garden, look carefully around the supermarkets for one that sells imported French maize-fed birds, recognisable by their yellow skin. They are a little more expensive than the ubiquitous unidentified clucking object, but for taste they are much superior and well worth the extra you pay.

Serves 4

1 × 3 lb (1.4kg) chicken
Oil
Salt and pepper

For the stuffing:
The chicken liver
2 cooked sausages, chopped
4 cooked slices smoked bacon, chopped
8 small pieces of toast
1 clove garlic, crushed
1 branch of thyme
1 bay leaf

Season the inside of the bird with salt and pepper.

Mash the stuffing ingredients together with your hands and fill the chicken. Then stitch up the hole so that the stuffing cannot escape. Thread the chicken onto the spit and secure. Oil the bird and cook for 1¼ hours, until the skin is crisp and the chicken is perfectly cooked. Serve with a bitter salad of chicory, dandelion leaves and radicchio, well turned in crushed garlic, olive oil and salt.

Spit-Roast Chicken

Serves 4

1 × 4 lb (1.8kg) chicken
2 teaspoons salt
2 medium-sized apples, peeled, cored and quartered
2 oz (50g) celery leaves
Lemon sauce (see page 35)

Rub the cavity of the chicken with salt and put the apple and celery leaves into it. Sew up the cavity with string and a skewer.

Fasten the neck skin to the skewer and tie the wings to the body. Insert a spit through the chicken and fix securely.

Cook the chicken for at least 1½ hours, or until the skin is brown and crispy and beginning to split. Baste regularly with the lemon sauce. Carve and serve with the remainder of the sauce, heated.

Chicken Breasts 'Two Rivers'

This is not really a classic dish, but is one that an imaginary centuries-old settlement of mandarins, inhabiting an area between the River Hi Po and the Bristol Avon, would have prepared for visiting colour-supplement food writers.

Serves 2

▓ 2 chicken breasts, skinned and halved

For the marinade:
2 spring onions, finely chopped
3 garlic cloves, crushed
4 teaspoons red bean paste (available from Oriental food shops)
1 tablespoon sesame seed oil
1 tablespoon sesame seeds
1 tablespoon sugar
1 tablespoon soy sauce
Black pepper

Flatten the chicken breasts with the flat side of a heavy knife. Score the flesh.

Combine all the ingredients to make the marinade, coat the chicken breasts all over and leave for 1 hour.

Grill for at least 5 minutes on each side.

Spiced Chicken

On a sailing holiday once, I found myself stranded in Motril in southern Spain with no money and no food. For several days I lived off the dabs that I could catch in the harbour. Delicious as these were, I was very pleased when a fellow sailor invited me to a beach party. Strange chap, also waiting for money to arrive, he was living on a rotting 'gun boat', the sort of thing they used to send up the Yangtse river. He was some kind of ex-patriate who, after a lifetime in Africa, found he couldn't really settle in the UK and so just drifted from place to place with three beautiful black ladies and a Somali cook, eating the most amazingly spiced food. This is one of their dishes, except that they used a pestle and mortar, naturally, rather than a liquidiser. I ate this dish till I was fit to burst it was so good. As was the fresh lime juice we drank for reasons of finance rather than principle!

Serves 6

1 × 3-4 lb (1.4-1.8kg) chicken, jointed
1 lb (450g) sweet red peppers, sliced and de-seeded
4 oz (110g) fresh red chillis, sliced and de-seeded
4 fl oz (110ml) olive oil
Juice of 1 lemon
Salt

Cook the peppers, both sweet and hot, in salted boiling water until tender. Then purée them in a blender. Mix the olive oil and lemon juice into the purée and add salt as necessary. Allow to cool.

Rub the spicy sauce all over the chicken joints and leave overnight.

Grill the chicken pieces for about 40 minutes, turning from time to time. Serve with a green salad.

Chicken Kebabs

Why not give your liver a rest and make jugs of iced yoghurt and milk whisked together and seasoned with salt, and quaff this creamy drink with the kebabs? It's terrific.

Serves 4

1 × 3 lb (1.4kg) chicken

For the marinade:
1 clove crushed garlic
3 fl oz (75ml) olive oil
½ teaspoon cayenne pepper
¼ teaspoon cumin
1 tablespoon lemon juice
½ teaspoon tomato purée
Salt and pepper

Wash and dry the chicken. Remove the skin and cut the flesh into cubes.

Mix all the marinade ingredients in a large bowl and add the chicken pieces, making sure that all the pieces are covered with the marinade. Leave for 2 hours.

Thread the chicken onto skewers and grill for about 10 minutes, turning frequently. Serve with rice and salad.

Chicken Kebabs with Oregano

Serves 4

4 chicken breasts, cut into cubes
1 slice thick ham, cut into cubes
1 red pepper, cut into cubes

For the marinade:

Juice of 1 lemon
3 tablespoons oil
1 clove garlic, crushed
1 teaspoon oregano
Salt and pepper

Mix the marinade ingredients together, add the chicken and ham and leave for at least 1 hour.

Thread the chicken, ham and red pepper onto skewers and grill for about 8 minutes, basting from time to time with the marinade. Serve with a piquant sauce of your choice (see sauce section) and saffron rice.

Chicken and Vegetable Kebabs

Serves 6

1 × 3 lb (1.4kg) chicken, cut into small pieces
6 chicken livers, halved or quartered
4 leeks (white part only), cut into 1 in (2.5cm) pieces
1 onion, coarsely chopped for a skewer
2 sweet green peppers, de-seeded and cut into small pieces
1 clove garlic, finely chopped
4 fl oz (110ml) soy sauce
4 tablespoons dry sherry
4 tablespoons sake
2 teaspoons sugar
¼ teaspoon cayenne pepper
1 in (2.5cm) fresh ginger root, finely chopped

Starting and ending with the chicken, arrange two chicken pieces and one piece each of liver, leek, onion and pepper onto oiled skewers.

Put the garlic, soy sauce, sherry, sake, sugar and cayenne pepper into a saucepan and bring to the boil. Pour over the skewered chicken and allow to marinate for about an hour.

Cook for 2-3 minutes, turning regularly. Then dip the skewers into the marinade again and grill for at least another 5 minutes.

Spit-Roast Guinea Fowl

My friend Harry decided to 'drop out' and buy a farm in Provence. Working on the principle that to make a small fortune you start with a large one, using various inheritances he decided to stock the farm with animals. I visited him one day to find him sitting on the terrace of the farm with a sleepy-looking guinea fowl in one arm and *Teach Yourself Chicken Rearing* in the other. The terrace was littered with half-finished glasses of wine and pastis from a party the night before – Harry's housekeeping left a lot to be desired. Anyway, the book gave no clue on how to deal with the ailing bird's symptoms – but I reckon that she had pecked away at the pastis and got drunk. At least she died happy. We ate her for supper.

Serves 2

1 young guinea fowl, trussed
4 sprigs of parsley
Paprika
Salt
2 oz (50g) melted butter or 4 tablespoons oil

Salt the cavity of the guinea fowl and put the parsley into it. Rub paprika all over the outside.

Thread the guinea fowl onto the spit and secure as necessary to stop it falling off! Cook for 40-50 minutes until it is evenly brown, basting regularly with melted butter or oil.

Grilled Poussins with Mustard

These little birds are so often tasteless when cooked in the normal way. Charcoal grilling them really improves their flavour.

Serves 6

3 poussins
1 oz (25g) butter
1 teaspoon mustard
Salt
Oil
Dry white breadcrumbs

Clean the poussins and split them in half, lengthwise, crushing them with a heavy knife, breaking the bones so that they lie flat while cooking. Brush the poussin pieces with oil and sprinkle with salt. Cook for about 10 minutes on each side on a hot grill.

Make a paste with the butter and the mustard. Spread the paste over the cooked poussins and sprinkle with breadcrumbs. Return to the grill and cook till golden brown.

Grilled Pheasant

This exquisitely simple dish should be prepared on one of those fine autumnal Sunday mornings when, clad in your green wellies and Barbour coat, you are tidying up the garden at the back end of the season. And instead of rushing to the pub after a morning's exercise, use the twigs and prunings of your fruit trees to make a fire. Imagine what the neighbours will think as you sit on your terrace amidst the apple-scented smoke spiralling upwards.

Serves 2

1 small pheasant
Salt and pepper
2 oz (50g) melted butter
4 oz (110g) breadcrumbs

While your wife makes a couple of strong hot toddies, cut the pheasant through its back and open it out flat. Smack it firmly with the side of your meat cleaver. Season with salt and pepper on both sides, paint it with the melted butter, tip it into the breadcrumbs and grill gently for 20 minutes on both sides. Paint it from time to time with more butter and take care it doesn't burn.

If you live in the area I imagine, there is almost certainly a stream at the bottom of your garden full of fresh watercress – this would make an excellent garnish for your pheasant along with a piquant sauce of your choice (see sauce section).

Merguez (on skewers) with Boudins and Apple Sauce (page 83)

Grilled Pigeons

Serves 4

4 pigeons, split open and flattened
Olive oil
Herbes de Provence
Salt and pepper

Brush the pigeons with olive oil and season with salt, pepper and the herbs.

Grill for 15 minutes per side, basting frequently with olive oil. Serve with tomatoes grilled with garlic and parsley and a tangy sauce (see sauce section).

Pink Pigeon Breasts with Chicory and Kumquats

Serves 2

Breasts of 4 pigeons (save the legs and carcasses in your deep freeze for a game pie)
Bigarade marinade (see page 29)
2 heads of chicory, blanched and separated into leaves
8 thin slices of speck (fat bacon)
8 kumquats (baby oranges available in many supermarkets)
1 glass red wine
1 tablespoon caster sugar
1 tablespoon crushed black peppercorns
4 oz (110g) smoked bacon, cubed

Marinate the pigeon breasts for 1 hour.

While the breasts are marinating, simmer the kumquats in red wine and sugar for 10 minutes.

Wrap the pigeon breasts in two chicory leaves and then in a slice of speck.

Pour the marinade, strained, and the juice from the cooked kumquats into à drip tray.

Thread the wrapped breasts, the smoked bacon cubes and the kumquats onto two skewers and grill for about 10 minutes.

Put the juices from the drip tray with the crushed peppercorns into a small saucepan and reduce the liquid by half. Strain this juice over the kebabs and serve with flat noodles.

Grilled Quails (page 106)

Grilled Quails

Serves 4

> 4 plump quails
> Salt and pepper
> 4 sprigs thyme
> 4 small knobs of butter
> 4 long slices of speck (fat bacon)
> 4 croûtons of lightly toasted bread, spread with butter and anchovy paste

You will need a fairly gentle fire for this cooking process.

Rub the salt and pepper inside each bird and push in a thyme sprig and a knob of butter. Wrap each one carefully and tightly with a strip of speck. Thread onto a skewer and roast gently, turning frequently for at least 30 minutes.

Just before serving, lift the birds off the fire, discard the speck and place them on the croûtons so that the last drops of fat from the birds are absorbed.

Quails with Mustard in Breadcrumbs

Serves 4

> 4 quails
> Salt and pepper
> 1 tablespoon parsley and tarragon, finely chopped
> 2 tablespoons prepared mustard
> 4 oz (110g) melted butter
> Fresh breadcrumbs to coat

Cut through the back of the birds with a knife and fold them open. Now smack them sharply with the palm of your hand or the flat of a meat cleaver so that they are well flattened.

Salt and pepper them on both sides and sprinkle with the herbs. Paste them with the mustard and dip them into the melted butter before pressing them on both sides into the breadcrumbs.

Grill them gently on both sides for a total of about 15 minutes, basting with the butter and making sure that they don't burn.

Grilled Rabbit

Serves 6-8

> 2 plump young rabbits, split in half and pounded flat
> Oil

For the basting mix:

1 clove garlic, crushed
Pinch of dried sage
3 tablespoons oil
2 tablespoons lemon juice
Salt and pepper

Brush the halved rabbits with oil and brown them on both sides over a very hot fire.

Then raise the rack over the fire and grill them more slowly for about 25 minutes. Mix the basting ingredients together. Baste the rabbits with the mixture, turning them often. Stick a sharp knife or skewer into the rabbits – they are cooked once the juices run clear.

Rabbit Kebabs with Mustard

Serves 4

1 rabbit, cut into 24 pieces

For the marinade:

4 tablespoons prepared strong mustard
4 fl oz (110ml) fresh cream
Salt and pepper

Remove the irritating little bones from the rabbit, leaving only the big ones.

Mix the marinade ingredients together and cover the rabbit pieces. Leave for 15 minutes.

Thread the bits onto skewers and grill for about 15 minutes, turning from time to time, basting with the marinade.

Jacket potatoes baked in the embers garnished with fresh chives and butter and any marinade left over will go very well with this dish.

Whenever you are roasting a chicken, or any bird for that matter, ensure that you have a drip tray underneath, because to get the crisp skin all round it must be basted frequently. There is no harm in putting a little alcohol into the drip tray along with a few herbs, thus enhancing the cooking juices, which you should use to baste the bird during the cooking process.

Venison Chops with Bacon

Serves 4

8 venison chops
8 slices of smoked bacon

For the marinade:
4 tablespoons oil
Juice of 1 lemon
1 tablespoon Worcester sauce
Salt and pepper

Mix the marinade ingredients together. Marinate the chops for 1 hour.

Now simply grill the chops for 5 minutes on each side and just before they are cooked, grill the bacon for a minute or two on each side.

If you are lucky enough to live next door to my mother. you would have spent the morning raiding her chestnut tree and preparing a purée of chestnuts to go with these delicious game chops. However, if you are unable to obtain fresh chestnuts, a purée of tinned chick peas with lots of pepper and melted butter will make a supreme accompaniment.

Venison and Apricot Kebabs

Serves 4

1 lb (450g) venison meat, diced into 1 in (2.5cm) cubes
Bigarade marinade (see page 29)
16 dried apricots, soaked in dry sherry
16 thin rashers of smoked bacon
16 thin slices of speck (fat bacon)
Salt and pepper

Marinate the cubed venison for at least 2 hours.

Wrap each apricot with smoked bacon and the venison with half a slice of speck. Thread onto four skewers.

Place a drip tray under the kebabs with the strained marinade and the juice from the apricots in it. Cook the kebabs for 15 minutes, gently so that the bacon does not burn before the meat is cooked, turning from time to time. Season with salt and pepper and serve with fresh pasta tossed in the juices from the drip tray.

VEGETABLES, FRUIT AND CHEESE

I am not and never will be a vegetarian; give me a man who eats caviare on impulse to one who eats brown rice on principle. Yet I can still feel sorry for those who have never enjoyed the pleasures of frosted sprouts fresh from the garden, cooked quickly in salted water, strained and eaten with melted butter and black pepper, tasting like soft-shelled walnuts. I can still pity those who hate them because some heathen from their childhood boiled them to a pale green pulp. I mourn for a generation compelled to eat frozen peas that has missed the delights of a plate of lightly cooked, freshly picked runner beans with melted butter, grated cheese and pepper; or a dish of tiny broad beans, parboiled, then tossed in bacon fat. Or what about aubergines cut into chips, dipped in flour and milk and deep-fried till they are crisp outside and like ripe bananas inside? A mountain of those and a bowl of piquant tomato sauce to dip them in; a bottle of wine and some bread and cheese – what a feast for a summer's day. Or the stunning colours of a ratatouille. Squeeze the courgettes in your mouth like boiled chestnuts in their skins, taste the caramel on the tomatoes sweet and slightly burnt, crunch a pepper and dip your bread into the olive oil. Van Gogh on a plate.

'But this a book of barbecues!' I hear you cry. Well, what about jacket potatoes on bonfire night: the delights of grilled red peppers, or tomatoes stuffed with chopped fresh herbs, basted with olive oil and baked under a dripping spit-roast chicken. Or chick peas, garlic and onions sizzling in a dish under spicy kebabs. Simple crisp salads, lightly tossed in olive oil to accompany the finest of grills. And as for roasting a great slab of hard cheese next to the coals and slicing off molten morsels and sucking them down with chunks or fresh bread, rather like a fondue, while sipping glasses of schnapps, well . . . Or perhaps hard goats' cheeses, marinated in olive oil and herbs and toasted crisp on the outside and soft like marshmallow inside. Or fruit kebabs, drenched in alcohol and dredged in sugar – wonderful.

Mushrooms with Garlic Butter

Come September the French go mad. Normally a gregarious race, shouting and swapping stories and drinks in the steamy bars, they suddenly change . . . they form themselves into little whispering groups and abruptly cease talking when a stranger or rival approaches. Wizened old men take out tatty bags from their leather overcoats and guardedly show the contents to a trusted friend.

It is the mushroom season. One of the greatest gastronomic events of the year. They skive off work and deceive their wives – to go mushroom collecting. They dream of returning with kilos of truffles. But seldom do.

One night in the Café de France, Léo, le patron, called me into his inner sanctum, the unkempt and cramped, dingy kitchen where he lived when not serving pastis to the customers. He closed the kitchen door behind him and conspiratorially, as if to reassure himself we were not being followed, he lifted a corner of the dirty net curtain of the kitchen door and peered into the bar. Satisfied that all was well he pulled open the kitchen table drawer and rummaged through 20 years of accumulated string, old candles, matches, can openers and pastis pourers and pulled out a twist of brown paper 3 or 4 inches in diameter. He pressed the package into my hand and said 'Don't tell anyone'. I started to open the package. He said 'Not now, save it until you get home.'

Léo had given me 3 dull black balls, like large walnuts and as black as coal. They were truffles. That night I had a feast which will stay in my memory for ever. I wrapped each truffle in caul and sprinkled it with salt and pepper before wrapping it again in tin foil. I placed the tin foil parcels in the edge of the embers of my fireplace for about 30 minutes. While they were cooking I toasted some hard-grained brown bread which I rubbed with garlic, toasted and dipped into virgin Provence olive oil. I ate the three truffles. They burned my fingers and delighted my soul as I dipped my toast into a bowl of Châteauneuf-du-Pape, alternately munching a corner and swigging a slurp. The sensation was as if the moon had kissed the earth.

But to get back to mushrooms, cèps, boletus etc, the following recipe is a simple way to grill the mushrooms of your choice.

AUTHOR'S NOTE: Please don't gather wild mushrooms without expert advice – I can't afford to lose readers.

Serves 4

- 12 cèps of the same size
- 2 tablespoons olive oil
- 3 oz (75g) softened butter
- 1 tablespoon parsley, chopped
- 2 cloves garlic, finely chopped
- Salt and pepper

Paint your mushrooms with olive oil and place them insides down on the grill for 7-8 minutes. During this time prepare the snail butter by mixing the garlic, parsley, salt, pepper and the butter. Turn the mushrooms onto their backs and fill each of them with some of the butter and cook for a further 4-5 minutes.

Mushrooms with Olive Oil and Fresh Herbs

Serves 4

- 12 mushrooms, with stalks removed
- 3 tablespoons olive oil
- Salt and pepper
- 2 cloves garlic, finely chopped
- 1 tablespoon parsley, finely chopped
- 1 teaspoon fresh oregano

Marinate the mushrooms in the oil, salt and pepper for 10 minutes. Grill the mushrooms for 10-15 minutes, depending on their size, turning from time to time. Mix together the garlic, parsley and oregano and spoon a little into each mushroom.

Stuffed Mushrooms

Serves 4

- 24 large mushroom caps
- 4 fl oz (110ml) olive oil
- 3 tablespoons lemon juice
- 2 tablespoons olive oil for cooking
- 1 sweet red pepper, de-seeded and finely chopped
- 5 cloves garlic, finely chopped
- 6 shallots, finely chopped
- 1 oz (25g) parsley, finely chopped
- 3 oz (75g) fresh white breadcrumbs
- Salt and pepper

Marinate the mushroom caps in the olive oil and lemon juice for at least 2 hours. Drain and keep the marinade on one side.

Heat the olive oil for cooking in a frying pan and sauté the pepper, garlic and shallots for about 5 minutes or until they are soft. Remove the pan from the heat and add the parsley, 4 tablespoons of the marinade and then stir in the breadcrumbs. Season with salt and pepper to taste and stuff the mushroom caps with the mixture.

Grill on an oiled rack for about 8-10 minutes, until they are well heated through.

Grilled Aubergines

A brilliant but simple way to eat aubergines is to grill them whole and unpeeled for about 20 minutes, turning them from time to time until their skin is black and they are very soft and squidgy. Then all you do is cut them in half and with a teaspoon mash in some olive oil, salt and pepper and spoon out the flesh rather as you would with an avocado pear.

A Vegetable Rainbow

Serves 4

1 red pepper, cut in quarters lengthways
1 green pepper, cut in quarters lengthways
2 aubergines, cut lengthways in slices ¾ in (2cm) thick
2 large tomatoes, quartered
Olive oil
Salt and pepper

Paint the vegetables liberally with oil, season with pepper and cook them for about 10 minutes, turning and oiling all the while. Once they are tender to touch they are tender to the tongue, so remove them from the grill, arrange them decoratively on a white serving dish, sprinkle with salt and a final splash of olive oil and eat.

Grilled Sweetcorn

Serves 4

Until I discovered this recipe I have never enjoyed fresh corn on the cob or even frozen corn on the cob. I am sorry to say that I always thought tinned corn on the cob was the best. But now my life has changed . . .

Simmer 4 young fresh yellow cobs in milk for about 15 minutes. Remove from the milk, paint with melted butter and put onto the grill for about 30 minutes, turning and basting with butter until they are golden. Eat at once with crushed sea salt and more melted butter.

Caramelised Bananas

I could go on forever extolling the virtues of these delightful fruit kebabs. What better way to pass a summer's evening than cooking dozens of these delights while drinking exotic cocktails and swapping pompous stories with your neighbours? However, on with the bananas . . .

Serves 4

4 bananas, not too ripe
4 oz (110g) caster sugar
½ teaspoon powdered cinnamon
½ teaspoon powdered vanilla
Large slug of whisky, Cognac or rum

Roll the bananas firmly in a mixture of the sugar, cinnamon and vanilla. Pop them onto the grill for 2 or more minutes until they are caramelised. Put them onto a serving dish and flame with the alcohol.

Fruit Kebabs

Serves 4

4 peaches, cut in half
4 apricots, cut in half
12 stoned black cherries
Large glass of apricot liqueur (or any other fruit liqueur)
4 oz (110g) caster sugar

Don't peel the fruit, but wash and dry it and put it to macerate in the liqueur for 10 minutes. Drain the fruit and don't throw the liqueur away – don't drink it either: you'll need it in a minute.

Prepare 4 kebabs by threading each one with half a peach, a cherry, half an apricot, a cherry etc. Now sprinkle them all liberally with sugar and pop them on the grill for 5-8 minutes or until they are beautifully caramelised.

Place them on a serving dish, heat the liqueur you've kept so carefully, pour it over the fruit kebabs and set fire to it. Obviously you could pour cream over them as well but to my mind this perfect drink on a stick, the very essence of summer, needs no further garnish.

Apple Kebabs

Serves 6

6 apples, peeled and cut into quarters
Juice of 1 lemon
2 oz (50g) melted butter
Caster sugar
Pot of double cream or clotted cream

Thread the apple quarters onto skewers, squeeze over the lemon juice, paint with melted butter, dip into sugar and grill for 5 minutes on each side or until they are well caramelised. Spoon on the thick yellow clotted cream and call for some iced dry cider.

Hawaiian Kebabs

These fruit kebabs are so mouthwatering, I could even consider becoming a vegetarian, while an endless supply of alcohol and a custom-built barbecue will be the two things I will insist on taking to my desert island. But I digress . . .

Serves 4

4 bananas, cut into quarters
4 lemons, cut into quarters
4 thick slices fresh pineapple, cut into quarters
Large glass rum
4 oz (110g) caster sugar

All you have to do is thread the fruit onto 4 skewers, dip them in the rum, sprinkle them liberally with sugar and cook for 5 minutes or so turning often and, if necessary, sprinkling with more sugar until it caramelises. Heat the rum and flame it over the kebabs and serve.

Grilled Goats' Cheeses

Serves 4

For hungry people this superbly simple recipe might be used as a starter or a savoury in a lengthy meal. For others, grilled cheeses served with toasted genuine wholemeal bread and a crisp salad of chicory, endives and radicchio, well dressed with good olive oil and garlic and washed down with chilled rosé, will make a delightful lunchtime or evening snack.

If you are lucky enough to buy unpasteurised individual French goats' cheeses while on holiday, or from a really good cheese shop at home, so much the better, but if all else fails buy the little banons which are wrapped in chestnut leaves and are available from most supermarkets. Or much better still, when you can buy a couple of dozen genuine ones (on holiday from a farm) preserve them by popping them into a Kilner jar with whole black peppercorns, a couple of dried chillis, a bay leaf or two and a few sprigs of rosemary and thyme, and then cover the lot with olive oil. Eat them raw or grilled at your will.

4 individual goats' cheeses, not too hard and not too soft
4 tablespoons olive oil
1 teaspoon coarse ground pepper
1 tablespoon rosemary spines

Cut a cross in both sides of the cheese and paint with the olive oil. Then press both sides of the cheese into a mix of the pepper and the rosemary spines. Grill lightly over the fire till they turn golden and start to ooze in the middle.

INDEX

A

Anchovies, Grilled, 45; Minute Steak with, 59; Spit-Roast Leg of Lamb with Vegetables, 63

Apple, Kebabs, 115; Liver and Apple Kebabs, 90

B

Bacon, Brochettes of Scallops with, 48-9; Chicken Liver Kebabs, 89; Lamb Chops with Mushroom Sauce, 65; Marinated Liver with, 89; Pork Kebabs with Green Peppercorns, 81; Sweetbread Kebabs with Madeira Sauce, 93; Veal and Kidney Kebabs, 84; Venison Chops with, 108

Bananas, Caramelised, 114; Fillet Steak with Rum and, 57; Hawaiian Kebabs, 115; Liver and Banana Kebabs, 88

Barbecues, equipment, 20-5

Bass Flamed with Fennel and Armagnac, 41

Beef, Beef Ball Kebabs, 62; Daube, 53-4; Fillet Steak with Blue Cheese, 56; Fillet Steak with Horseradish, 56-7; Fillet Steak with Rum and Bananas, 57; Fillet Steak with Shallot Butter, 58; The Gastronaut's Hamburger, 60-1; Marinated Steak, 60; Minute Steak with Anchovies, 59; Moroccan Kebabs, 75; Rib of Beef with Herbs, 55; Sirloin Steak with Wine Butter, 59; Sirloin with Mustard, 58; Spit-Roast Beef with Paprika, 54-5; Spit-Roasted Fillet of Beef with Cream and Pepper, 54

Bream, Baked in Sea Salt, 41-2; Sweet and Sour Kebabs, 42

Butter, Anchovy, 28; Garlic, 112; Lobster, 28; Maître d'Hôtel, 28; Mustard, 65-6; Orange, 66; Shallot, 58; Shrimp or Prawn, 28; Wine, 29, 59

C

Calf's Kidneys with Prunes, 92

Calf's Liver, Grilled, 88

Cheese, Beef Ball Kebabs, 62; Fillet Steak with Blue Cheese, 56; Grilled Goats' Cheeses, 115-16; Hamburgers, 61

Chicken, Breasts, 'Two Rivers', 98; Grilled Poussins with Mustard, 101-2; Kebabs, 99-100; Kebabs with Oregano, 100; Liver Kebabs, 89; Liver Kebabs with Madeira, 90-1; Roast Stuffed, 97; Spiced, 98-9; Spit-Roast, 97-8; and Vegetable Kebabs, 100-1

Cod Fillets with Lemon, 43

Crayfish, Grilled, 47-8

F

Fillet Steak, with Blue Cheese, 56; with Horseradish, 56-7; with Rum and Bananas, 57; with Shallot Butter, 58

Fish, 40-50; Grilled Mixed, 49; Unidentified Fish Parcels, 50; Whole Fish on the Spit, 50

Fruit, 114-15

G

Game and poultry, 96-108

Guinea Fowl, Spit-Roast, 101

H

Hamburgers, Cheese, 61; The Gastronaut's, 60-1

Harissa, 32

Hawaiian Kebabs, 115

Hearth cooking, 20-2

Hollandaise Sauce, 35

Horseradish, Fillet Steak with, 56-7

I

Indian Kebabs, 74

Indian Minced Lamb Kebabs, 73

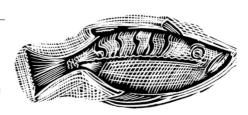